How to Get Started in Real Estate Investing

How to Get Started in Real Estate Investing

Robert Irwin

McGraw-Hill

New York   Chicago   San Francisco   Lisbon   London
Madrid   Mexico City   Milan   New Delhi   San Juan
Seoul   Singapore   Sydney   Toronto

McGraw-Hill

A Division of The **McGraw·Hill** Companies

9 0   DOC/DOC   0 9 8 7 6 5 4 3

ISBN 0-07-139649-7

Printed and bound by R. R. Donnelley & Sons Company.

This book contains the author's opinions. Some material in this book may be affected by changes in market conditions, or real estate law or the tax code (or changes in interpretations of the law or tax code). Hence, the accuracy and completeness of the information contained in this book cannot be guaranteed. Neither the author nor the publisher is engaged in rendering investment, legal, tax, accounting, or other similar professional services. If these services are required, the reader should obtain them from a competent professional.

McGraw-Hill books are available at special quantity discounts to use as premiums and sales promotions, or for use in corporate training programs. For more information, please write to the Director of Special Sales, Professional Publishing, McGraw-Hill, Two Penn Plaza, New York, NY 10121-2298. Or contact your local bookstore.

For other books by Robert Irwin, check out his website:
www.robertirwin.com

This book is printed on recycled, acid-free paper containing a minimum of 50% recycled, de-inked fiber.

CONTENTS

Preface

The first book I ever wrote was *How To Buy And Sell Real Estate For Financial Security* back in 1973. It was an immediate success and launched a second career for me of writing about real estate instead of only buying and selling it.

I always liked that first book because it laid out in the simplest possible way how to get started investing in real estate. Now, more than 60 books later, I'm returning to its concept. Again a young couple starts with a house and then begins buying more properties, one after another, until they build their fortune. It takes them step-by-simple-step through the process of investing in real estate, so any reader can easily see how it's done.

In this book, updated for a new century, I bring back Leo, the real estate agent who helps them get started. Without sleight of hand, he shows them how it's done from starting with a small house to live in, to moving on to sales and trades.

It's my hope that this new book will help launch many of you, its readers, into successful careers as real estate investors. And that you will make as much money and more as do it's lead characters, Leslie and David.

Robert Irwin

1

Real Estate Investing Step by Step

One of the most commonly asked questions in real estate is, "How do I get started?" For those on the outside looking in, real estate can seem a complex, even arcane field with strange rules and even stranger conventions.

To answer this question, most books I've read (including many of my own) offer a series of chapters explaining different aspects of the field. While this is certainly helpful, it's not really the hands on instruction that I suspect most beginners really crave.

Therefore, to help those new to the field get their feet wet, I've designed this first chapter in the form of a narrative. In it we'll follow a couple from the time they decide to purchase their first real estate investment—a house they will live in—through their first trades and more sophisticated property transactions. Of course, the characters described are fictional; they are drawn from many real estate investors I've known over the years. However, the situations they are in and the profits they make are indicative of what real people are doing in the field all the time.

If you are an experienced investor, you might prefer to proceed directly to later chapters. However, at some point you may want to return to this chapter to review the basics of investing in real estate. You may be surprised to find information here that you thought you knew but in fact aren't quite up on.

Making Choices to Get the Most from Your Real Estate Investments

David and Leslie wanted to get financially ahead in life. David was 31 and Leslie was 28. They hoped to make enough money to retire comfortably within 20 years.

They had already tried buying stocks, but they had lost their investment in the market crashes of the early 2000s. Because of their bad experience, David felt that all investments were inherently risky, and he wanted to simply put their money in the bank. Leslie was more adventuresome and wanted to try other investment venues. In addition, although they lived in a comfortable apartment, they also wanted to move up to a house where they would have more privacy, more space, and more control over their environment.

Thus, they turned their attention to buying a combination shelter/investment house. The combination of investing their money and improving their living situation seemed to be a lot safer than buying stocks and it seemed to make for a much more stable future.

The spur came when they learned from their accountant that if they owned a home, they could deduct all of their property taxes plus the interest on their mortgage. (None of their apartment rent was deductible, for them.) No other investment offered this type of tax relief. Thanks to help from the government in the form of deductions, making the house payments would be far easier than they had at first thought.

So they set out to find their first real estate purchase—a house to live and invest in.

David and Leslie were immediately faced with lots of choices for their first real estate investment. They could purchase a single-family house or a condo/co-op. They could buy near to work or far away. They had dozens of neighborhoods to choose from. They wondered:

- Where should we buy for the best investment?
- What kind of a home should it be?
- How big should it be?
- Should it be new or a resale?
- Will all homes be equal as investments?

Trying to find answers, they visited several Realtors®. [A Realtor is a member of the National Association of Realtors (NAR), a trade organization that promotes better business practices.] One of the Realtors they visited, Leo, was an old hand, having been in the business for over 30 years.

He took Leslie and David under his wing and explained some of the insights he had gathered. The first thing he said about investing in property was, "You make your profit when you buy, not when you sell."

When Leslie and David looked at each other with puzzled expressions, Leo explained that profit was, basically, the difference between their purchase price and their sales price (less, of course, costs). While they certainly would try to buy a home as inexpensively as possible, if they bought the right property, they could boost the other end of the equation, the selling price, thus increasing their margin of profit.

"What I'm saying is simply that when buying for profit, you should think less about what you would ideally want in a house and much more about what the next buyers will want."

Leo used the "four-out-of-five rule." "If four out of five buyers will like something about a home, that feature will help resell it, even if you personally dislike the feature. If only one out of five will like it (even if that one is you), it's going to hold the home's resale back—reduce the price and take longer to sell. "Take paint as an example," Leo said. "You may not particularly care for light colors. But most buyers do like them. Therefore a light-colored home will sell faster and for more than, for example, a home colored in dark grays or browns.

"In other words," Leo concluded, "for an investment, plan your resale when you buy by looking for what most other buyers will want."

Leslie nodded in agreement, but David wasn't sure. He asked Leo to give some examples of the features that four out of five buyers were looking for. Leo listed the following.

Features to Look for When Buying an Investment (or Any) Home

Good Neighborhood Schools

Leo pointed out that nothing made a home more a valuable investment than having good neighborhood schools. Studies repeatedly showed that the better the schools, the faster and higher home prices appreciated. Indeed, in areas where schools were poor, home prices sometimes went the other way, down!

TIP

You can find out about the quality of nearby schools by simply giving school districts a call. They all have standardized test scores that are available to the public. Also, many Web sites offer these statistics.

Pride-of-Ownership Evident in the Neighborhood

This time Leslie was puzzled. She said she certainly had heard of this, but she found it hard to understand. Leo said it was easier to see than to describe. When all the homes in a neighborhood are well painted and well landscaped, and there is no trash out front (or cars being worked on), it indicates that the neighbors are proud of their homes. Buying a home in this kind of well-kept neighborhood would pay good dividends later on (would make a wise investment) both when Leslie and David bought a home and, importantly, when they resold it. Leslie nodded. David seemed unconvinced. He liked to work on his car in the front yard.

Low Crime Rate in the Neighborhood

Leo pointed out that David and Leslie naturally didn't want to live in a high crime area. But they probably hadn't really given it much thought. Leo now emphasized how important it was. He pointed out that while no area is completely safe, many areas have significantly lower crime rates than others. People with families as well as singles and couples prefer the low crime areas. David nodded in agreement here. Leslie didn't seem to think it was that important. Leo then asked, "How would you like to try to collect rents in a high-crime area? As we go, you may want to someday rent out the house you're now buying. Someone might be out there ready to steal your hard-earned profits from you before you got home." Leslie admitted that when Leo put it that way, it made a lot of sense.

Leo said he had his own way of telling how crime ridden a neighborhood is. He called it his "graffiti index." The more graffiti on the walls and fences, the worse the crime in the area. On the other hand, where neighbors quickly paint over graffiti or it seldom appears, there is generally less crime and less gang activity.

TIP

You can learn about the crime rate in an area by calling the public affairs officer of the local police department, which often provides crime statistics not only by neighborhood but by street and block as well.

Close to Shopping and Access to Transportation

Leo pointed out that these days when traffic congestion is a major concern, having access to freeways, busses, trains, and other forms of transportation is a big issue. Homes that have this access are considered far more desirable, both for owners and for potential tenants, than those that do not. Leslie said that she wanted a place that was close to where David worked (he was an engineer in a food processing plant), so he wouldn't have a long commute. David said that their house should be located somewhere between their two jobs. (Leslie was an elementary school teacher.) Leo said that being somewhere between the two workplaces was a good idea for their first home. Their second real estate investment, however, should be close to the first.

Minimum House Size

"How big a house do you want?" Leo asked. Leslie and David looked at each other and said, "Big enough, but not too big." Leo said that most people feel the same way. That preference translates to at least three bedrooms and two baths with a minimum of about 1,800 square feet. "You'll be comfortable in a house that size, and chances are that others will be too when it comes time to resell."

"Okay," David said. "Let's be sure I understand what you're saying. We should look for a home with the five qualities you just described."

TIP

Here's a list of qualities to look for when buying an investment (or any) home:

1. Good neighborhood schools
2. Pride-of-ownership evident in the neighborhood
3. Low crime rate in the neighborhood
4. Close to shopping and access to transportation
5. Minimum house size

Additional Features to Look for When Buying an Investment Home

"But," David continued, "those are things anyone would look for when buying a home to live in. What about the special features you mentioned that are peculiar to investment homes?"

Leo nodded. You'll want to look for additional qualities in your home purchase." He pointed out that real estate investments have to be rented out to produce income. Hence, any home that David and Leslie purchased should have those qualities that would make it a good rental down the road. "Eventually, you're going to want to rent out that house as an investment. So it needs to be attractive to good tenants."

Leo pointed out that a rental would need to have not only the five principal characteristics just mentioned but also the following three.

An Active Rental Market in the Area

Leo pointed out that some areas have a lot of well-paid workers, yet a shortage of housing. This makes for an excellent tenant pool. Other areas have lots of housing, but relatively few people who want (or can afford) to live there.

Thus, in addition to investigating the area in which they were considering buying a home to be sure it was a good location for resale, they would also need to investigate to be sure the area had a good rental market as well.

David looked skeptical. "How could we possibly know that?" Leo smiled and said, "I, or any other active agent, could quickly tell you since most of us handle rentals as well as sales." He pointed out that David and Leslie could also check for themselves by looking in the local paper under "homes for rent," calling some of the landlords, chatting with them, and visiting some of the rental properties. Very quickly they'd find out how well rentals were doing and what types of properties were available. "It's simply a matter of immersing yourself in the rental market until you have a feel for it."

A House That Is Suitable for Renting

Leo pointed out that while it is commonly believed that any home can be rented out (as indeed it could), some homes, because of their size and design, made far better rentals than others. Indeed, some homes are badly suited to be rentals.

"You want a house that isn't too big so you won't attract tenants with lots of kids. According to the Fair Housing Act, you can't refuse to rent to families with children. But the house size will determine how many children will fit into it."

Leo pointed out that a five-bedroom house can accommodate far more kids than a three-bedroom house. But five bedrooms won't generate much more rent, and the small amount of additional rent won't compensate for the wear and tear caused by so many people living in one house. Therefore, the best rental home is generally a three-bedroom house, with a four-bedroom house following. Anything more is simply asking for rental trouble.

"In addition," Leo pointed out, "you usually don't want a house with expensive fixtures or features. Because it's not their property, tenants simply won't take as good care of the property as you will. Stained-glass windows, elaborate chandeliers, white carpeting, and so on are all no-no's. You want a home that will stand up to wear and tear."

TIP

Some investors specialize in high-end properties. If you eventually get to that stage, you will then want homes with expensive amenities. However, you will also then be getting substantially more rent and a much bigger damage deposit.

A House That Is Easily Maintained

Finally, Leo pointed out that they would want a rental that wouldn't need a lot of upkeep and maintenance. "The expense of fixing a roof or a water heater or an air-conditioning system can turn a profitable rental into an 'alligator.'"

Both Leslie and David laughed. Leo continued, "You haven't heard of a real estate alligator? When the payments on your rental property are too high, they become an alligator that will eat you alive. Your goal is to at least break even. That means that the rent (plus tax advantages, which Leo said he would describe later) pays for your mortgage, taxes, insurance, and other costs. That may be possible, unless you have big maintenance and repair problems. Those expenses can quickly throw you into a negative situation, an alligator."

"All homes need repair and maintenance," David pointed out sternly.

"True," Leo said. "But the younger the home, the less likely it will need work." He explained that homes less than seven years old rarely need to have water heaters replaced, furnaces and air-conditioners fixed, roofs repaired, and so on. He said that the ideal rental property is less than seven years old.

"Okay," said Leslie. "To summarize, that means that we're looking for a home that also has the three additional qualities you just described."

TIP

Here's a list of additional qualities to look for when buying an investment home:

6. An active rental market in the area

7. A house that is suitable for renting

8. A house that is easily maintained

Leo nodded. But David had a scowl on his face. "What you're saying," he began, "is that we might have to give up something we like if we're going to look for a good investment property."

Leslie looked surprised and asked what David meant. He replied that suppose they found a cute little home that was perfect for them. It had two or five bedrooms. It had some ornate wooden banisters. It had expensive white carpeting and fancy imported tile work in the kitchen. In short, it would make a perfect home for them. However, it might not be suitable for tenants who would not have a vested interest in the property and therefore might not take very good care of it.

"So you're saying we need to give up some of what we might want to have in order to buy a property that will be better suited to renting."

Leslie looked at Leo. Leo nodded and said, "That's how you make your profit."

Leslie seemed surprised. "Well," she said, "why not buy a home for ourselves and then, later on, buy a rental?"

"The most important reason," said Leo, "is the financing."

Both Leslie and David looked puzzled and said in unison, "The financing?"

Yes, explained Leo. He noted that the best financing was available for owner-occupied property. The worst was available for investor-purchased property. "You can get a loan for 95 percent of the value of the home if you intend to live in it. If you have excellent credit and sufficient income, that loan amount can go up to 97 percent. In some cases it can be 100 percent or even 103 percent (where the mortgage actually pays most of your closing costs).These are "conforming" loans which currently have a maximum of $307,000, although that goes up frequently."

On the other hand, Leo pointed out, if you're buying as an investment, the best financing you're likely to get requires you to put at least 10 percent down and pay all of your closing costs. "If you decide on a $200,000 home, that means that if you occupy it, you can get into it with virtually no cash of your own. If you buy to rent it out, it will cost you at least $20,000 down *plus* closing costs."

TIP

The rule when buying real estate for investment is to do so with other people's money (OPM). Use as much of other people's money to make the purchase as you can. That will help you to maximize (*leverage*) your profits and minimize your exposure to risk.

"We have only about $10,000 saved, so getting in with as little cash as possible is a necessity," Leslie said. David nodded in agreement.

"That's why you need to make some sacrifices," Leo pointed out. "You buy a home that you can later rent out as an investment and sell for a profit. That means that instead of buying the home of your dreams, you compromise and buy one that you can stand to live in but that later will make a good rental and sale. Remember, you're not going to stay there forever."

TIP

The average home owner lives in a home for around eight years. The average investor seeking to maximize his or her real estate profits stays in a home for two years.

"Okay, that's settled," said Leslie. "When do we begin looking!"

Finding the First Home

Leo said he'd prepare a list of homes for them to see, which he did, and the next day they went out looking. They lived in the Sacramento, California, area and home prices at the time ranged from a low of around $150,000 to a high of about $350,000. (Of course, there were homes beyond either end of that range, but those tended to be either in very undesirable neighborhoods or super-expensive areas.) Given their combined income, which was under $100,000 a year, Leo suggested they look for a home around $200,000, which they could afford to finance. He pointed out that there were lots of very nice neighborhoods near where they worked and many suitable homes.

Leslie pondered that statement, then asked if higher-priced or lower-priced homes appreciated faster, and were better for resale? Leo said it depended on the residential real estate market cycle. Generally, after a slowdown, higher-priced homes are the first to go up in the price. At the middle or near the end of a recovery, it is the middle- to lower-priced homes that increase most in value.

TIP

Like other areas of the economy, real estate also has its ups and downs. Between 1990 and 1998, prices of residential real estate dropped as much as 30 percent in some areas of the country. Between 1998 and 1991, prices soared as much as 60 percent, often in the same areas!

David asked if higher- or lower-priced homes made better rentals? Leslie nodded that she wanted to know too.

High Priced or Low Priced?

Leo replied that most real estate investors in the past preferred modestly priced homes as rentals. He pointed out that lower-priced homes usually offered a bigger tenant base to select from. Also, they were easier to get into simply because they were cheaper—less money down, lower mortgage payments.

However, the real estate boom of the late 1990s and early 2000s changed that. At that time the higher-priced properties took off in value. Price appreciation was strongest at the top end, and investors bought the highest-priced homes they could afford. They rented them out ruthlessly and often sold within a short time. Some even "flipped" their properties.

Leslie asked, "Flipped?"

Leo explained, "Sold them for a profit before they ever took possession." He said they would look into that in detail shortly.

However, those heady days were relatively short-lived, and property appreciation slowed in most areas. Also, it spread down the scale to the lower-priced homes. "Probably the safest investment is a middle-of-the-road home. You can get into it without straining too much, and if it takes a while for it to appreciate in value, you won't have trouble holding onto it as a rental."

David nodded and said that after their horrendous experience in the stock market, safety was a primary issue.

Leo nodded too, but he had a twinkle in his eye. "After you get your feet wet, I'm sure you'll be making much more adventuresome purchases."

David suddenly asked if they should look for a condo.

Both Leo and Leslie looked at him in surprise. "Why a condo?" she asked.

Condo Unit or Detached Single-Family House?

David looked smug and replied, "Because I've heard you can buy a condo for a fraction of the price of a single-family home, yet it's in the same neighborhood. Why pay more when you can get the same thing for less?" He looked proud of himself. Leslie looked at Leo questioningly.

"Actually," Leo said, "you're partly correct. A condo of the same square footage is, indeed, normally cheaper than a house. But there's a reason. Condos tend to appreciate slower than single-family homes. And there can be problems when it comes time to rent them out."

TRAP

Historically, condos are the first to lose value in a real estate recession and the last to go up in price during an expansion.

"What kinds of problems?" Leslie asked.

Leo pointed out that all condominiums have a home owner's association (HOA). It establishes rules that often act as road blocks to landlords. For example, it might prohibit individual owners from posting for-rent signs in front of the building. Often there are also parking, noise, and occupancy restrictions.

"It's important to understand," Leo said, "that a condo is not simply a cheaper type of house. It's a different lifestyle." Occupants usually share common walls, ceilings, and floors. They share pools and other recreation areas. The landscaping in front of the units is handled by the HOA and cannot usually be altered. You usually can't even change the exterior paint. In short, in a condo you give up some independence for the community good." Usually this shared type of lifestyle works best with owner-occupants who agree to live by its standards. It can be a problem for tenants who don't have a vested interest in the sharing but only want habitation and to be left alone.

TRAP

Co-ops are even more restrictive than condos. Often the board that governs the co-op will insist on financially approving any tenants. Sometimes, although the practice is usually illegal, that interference extends to approving the tenants themselves. Some co-ops simply don't want any tenants in the building.

"In other words," Leslie said, "you're saying that later on we could have trouble renting out the condo."

Leo nodded, "You could rent it out. But it might be more difficult—take more time and produce a lower rental rate than a similarly sized single-family home. And, when you went to sell, you probably would make less of a profit than you would if you had purchased a single-family home."

Leslie looked at David and said pointedly, "No condo." He nodded meekly, then asked, "What about fixer-uppers? I've heard we can get a real bargain on those."

In Need of Serious Repair, or Ready for Moving In?

Leo nodded. He pointed out that many people made an excellent living doing nothing more than moving into a run-down property, fixing it up, and selling it for a profit. "For some, it's their full-time job, and they're quite successful at it. However," he continued, "for beginning investors like you, it probably isn't the wisest choice. It would make more sense for you to get a few homes under your belt before branching out into fixer-uppers (also called "handy-man specials" in some parts of the country)."

David shook his head stubbornly. "We learn quickly. I'm sure we can do whatever's necessary."

Leo nodded, "I'm sure you can. But why tackle a bear when you can first catch a rabbit?" He pointed out that there were inherent difficulties in buying a fixer-upper. Leslie nodded, and so did David, grudgingly. No fixer-upper.

TRAP

The following is a list of some of the difficulties likely to arise in purchasing a fixer-upper:

1. It's hard to know how much to pay. Only someone skilled in renovation will know what the true costs of fixing it up will be. The most common mistake made by novices is paying too much for a property. When they find out how much it really costs to fix it up, they discover they're way over market value. (See Robert Irwin's book, *Tips and Traps When Renovating Your Home,* McGraw-Hill, 2000.)

2. Sellers of fixer-uppers typically want much too much for their properties. Sellers often want what their property will be worth after it's fixed up. But they're selling it in run-down condition. That means that for every 10 fixer-upper properties you see, you may be able to get only one at a realistic price, and then only after much haggling with the seller over price.

3. The financing can be difficult. It's very unlikely you'll get one of those no-down/low-down mortgages we were speaking of on a fixer-upper. More likely, lenders will shy away because the property is in such bad shape. Instead, they'll demand you put more of your money in. That's the opposite of what you want.

The House on Horizon Drive

Armed with all of the investment information imparted by Leo, Leslie and David began a search of homes in their area. They looked for property in neighborhoods as close to their employment as possible.

TRAP

Everyone changes jobs over the years. However, the smartest real estate investors will try to find new employment near the old so they can continue to be near their properties and handle tenant, maintenance, and repair problems. If your job is going to require you to travel often or to frequently move to far-away locations, you might be better off *not* investing in real estate!

Since they were in Sacramento, they had a large supply of homes to choose from. The southern part of the city had a large number of industrial plants with a good supply of workers making solid wages, so the tenant base was sound. Most of the homes were modestly priced (around or under $250,000 at the time). New homes were constantly being built, but they tended to be higher in price than the resales.

TIP

Some of the best real estate investment properties are located in blue-collar areas. These workers, who often have steady well-paying jobs, will often opt to rent rather than buy. On the other hand, some investors do very well in specialty markets such as top-end properties ($750,000 and higher). But in this market the investor must be able to afford to buy these properties in the first place; unless already well-heeled, they can be difficult for new investors to purchase.

The house they ultimately found was on Horizon Street. It was one of a tract of around 250 homes, all similar, all roughly the same size. It had four bedrooms and two and a half baths. The asking price was $189,000.

Leo suggested they check out the house against the list of eight features he had said to look for when buying a home both to live in and invest in.

Features to Look for When Buying Any Home

1. *Good neighborhood schools.* Scores were in the 70th percentile—not as good as top areas but good enough to attract tenants and future buyers with children.

2. *Pride-of-ownership evident in the neighborhood.* The neighborhood was four years old, and owners had put in lawns, trees, and shrubs. Everything was well kept with no broken-down cars in driveways and no yards filled with weeds. Again, attractive to both owners and tenants.

3. *Low crime rate in the neighborhood.* The crime rate was typical for the overall area, neither especially high nor especially low. The police department revealed that the crime rate in the neighborhood and on their block was stable—mainly a couple of robberies and stolen cars over a year's time. There was no graffiti anywhere to be seen. There would be no problem collecting rents!

4. *Close to shopping and access to transportation.* Shopping was a minor problem. The nearest grocery store was about 10 minutes away, and the nearest mall, about 20 minutes away—not as close as might be desired but not overly distant. The neighborhood was within five minutes of a freeway on-ramp, which was excellent. Adequate for both tenant and owner.

5. *Minimum house size for the rental market.* The home was 1,800 square feet. It had four bedrooms, which meant that the living areas were necessarily small. Nevertheless, it would be quite suitable for a tenant. And since it was two levels, it looked more spacious than it actually was.

Additional Features to Look for When Buying an Investment Home

6. *An active rental market in the area.* They checked the local papers for rental ads, and they found that there were several other similar properties being rented out. They discovered that, based on what other owners were getting, they could reasonably expect to rent the home for around $1,300 a month. If they rented it for

slightly less, they could expect to rent it quickly and keep it full almost all the time. Leo said that this rental income would work out well with their payments and after-tax benefits. Leo also pointed out that it was a good rental area because of the large number of working people at nearby plants.

TIP

One of the keys to making money on rentals is to avoid changing tenants often. And one of the best ways to keep tenants is to charge slight less than market price.

7. *A house that is suitable for renting.* The home was relatively "plain." It had no ornate chandeliers or delicate banisters. The carpeting was dark beige, which wouldn't show dirt easily. The front yard was small and could be easily maintained. The biggest problem was the big backyard. It would require lots of maintenance. However, Leo pointed out that at the very least, David and Leslie could simply put in a sprinkler system and plant lawn. It would look green and require only mowing, which either the tenant or David could handle. "Rear yards usually don't have to be special for rentals, or even for sales," Leo said.

8. *A house that is easily maintained.* Since the house was only four years old, it was unlikely it would have many problems. Nevertheless, Leo insisted that they have it thoroughly inspected and have the sellers pay for a home warranty plan that would cover most problems for at least a year.

Getting Ready to Make an Offer

Leo stressed that before David and Leslie could hope to have an offer accepted by a seller, they had to prove to that seller that they could afford to make the purchase. "The way you do that is to get a *preapproval letter* from a lender saying just what you can afford in terms of the loan amount and monthly payments."

   Leo sent them to a mortgage broker who took an application and asked them to pay a fee of $35 for a credit check. Then the loan broker submitted their application, credit check, verification of their income, and cash-on-deposit to a lender. Within a short time the lender sent back a letter stating exactly the maximum monthly payment they could afford and committing itself to giving them a mortgage. With that, and using the current interest rates, anyone could calculate their maximum loan.

TIP

Mortgage brokers can be easily found anywhere in the country. You can check the Yellow Pages, but it's better if you can get a recommendation from someone you trust. Be sure you *don't* pay a big fee upfront to the mortgage broker. And be aware that the preapproval letter should come directly from the lender, not the mortgage broker.

   As it turned out, David and Leslie could afford a mortgage of up to $190,000 with as little as 3 percent down. If they held their closing costs to 2 percent, they had just enough cash to make the deal. (If the closing costs were higher, they could get a 100 percent mortgage, but the interest rate and monthly payments would also be slightly higher.)

   The only downside was that because the loan was going to be for more than 80 percent of the value of the property, they would be required to pay *private mortgage insurance* (PMI). This insured the lender against loss should Leslie and David not make the payments. The PMI amounted to an additional one-half percent in interest, boosting the payment about $100 a month.

Making the Offer

Leslie and David were ready to offer the full asking price of $189,000. However, Leo said that they should at first try low-balling the seller. The agent had disclosed that the home had been on the market for two months and had not had any previous offers. "Let's see how much less they are willing to take," Leo suggested.

So they offered 15 percent less than the asking price. Their offer was for $161,000.

"That's awfully low," worried David. Leslie looked to Leo.

"Yes it is," he said. "And by offering less than the asking price, you have to be prepared to walk away from the property. The sellers might not accept. They might not even counter. You might lose a potential deal.

"On the other hand, if things do go badly, there are many other properties to choose from in this area. It's a good investment offer."

TRAP

Investors must not be swayed by sentiment (fall in love with a home). They must be prepared to try offers on many properties in order to get one at a good price.

Leo prepared the offer, and they signed it. Just before Leo left to present it, Leslie asked, "You're giving the sellers only until 12:00 tonight to accept. That's only seven hours away. Shouldn't we give them more time? What if they have other commitments and can't consider the offer right away?"

Leo smiled and said, "Time is of the essence in real estate. You want to put the sellers on the spot. You want to make them commit one way or another. Giving them more time just allows for another offer to slip in from another buyer. Or for the sellers to waffle. Either they'll accept your offer, counter it, or reject it. You'll know soon enough."

TIP

Never (or almost never—there are always special circumstances!) give the sellers more than 24 hours to accept an offer. Make time work for you and against the other party.

Leslie and David went back to their apartment. They watched television, but they stayed near the phone waiting for Leo to call. He called at 9:30.

"There's good new and bad news," he said. "They've rejected your price. But they countered at a price that's lower than they were asking. I'll be right over to explain their counteroffer."

Fifteen minutes later Leo arrived. The sellers had countered at $179,000. That was $10,000 less than their asking price. Both David and Leslie were jubilant. They wanted to sign right away.

"If you were just buying to live in the house and were in love with it, I'd probably suggest you do sign," Leo said. "But, you want to be investors. And as such, you don't want to 'leave any money on the table.' You want to get the lowest possible price. So I suggest you counteroffer, knowing full well it could mean you'll lose the deal, but hoping you'll get a better price."

TIP

A counteroffer means the party rejects the current offer and is making a new one. The first party is no longer bound by their original offer. They can simply refuse the counter and walk away. You can't *both* accept an offer and counter it.

"Why don't you come up a bit, say, $5,000, and see what the sellers do?" Leo suggested.

Leslie and David both looked worried, but they agreed. After Leo left, David asked, "Maybe we're making a mistake. After all, the sellers dropped the price a lot."

Leslie replied, "Yes, so they probably want to get out badly. Maybe they'll drop it more. Remember, we're 'investors' now." David nodded, but he still looked worried.

At 11:30 Leo called to see if they were still up. They were, waiting by the phone. He said he'd be right over.

He was there 15 minutes later. The sellers had rejected their offer but had countered at $175,000. Leo said, "They really didn't want to come down anymore, but I told them you were investors who would just as easily walk away. So they grudgingly came down $4,000. I doubt they'll budge a penny more.

"Now you have to decide whether the price is right for you and either accept this counteroffer, or counter again and be prepared to lose the deal."

Leslie said, "When we checked comparable sales, homes like this one in the area were selling for between $185,000 and $190,000. This price is at least $10,000 less. It's hard to see how we could go wrong. Let's do it." David seemed less convinced, but he agreed. Without further ado, they had bought the home on Horizon Drive.

On to Bigger and Better Things!

Leslie and David had been living in Horizon Drive for over a year. During that time they put in a backyard patio and overhang, and they repainted as needed. They enjoyed home keeping, but they still had it in mind to invest. They had saved $6,000 by then, and they decided it was time to make another move in real estate. Almost 15 months to the day later, they called Leo.

Leo said it was a good time to invest. Property prices had been going up. He did a comparative market analysis (CMA) on their home, and they discovered that their home, for which they had paid $175,000, was now worth well over $200,000.

"I hadn't realized it had gone up so fast," Leslie said. Leo reminded them that they had bought the house the right way, coming in at a low-ball figure and getting the house for below market price. The gain in the market value of their house and a year's worth of price appreciation had boosted their home's value.

TIP

It's not necessary to buy a property at a low price to make a profit if you're willing to hold onto it for a while. In most areas, inflation and the national housing shortage (in many areas) will work in your favor to raise the market value and produce a profit for you—just hang onto it long enough.

David was skeptical about investing, however, since they had only $6,000 in savings.

Leo smiled and said, "You've got a lot more than that. You've got all of that equity in your home." Leo suggested they call their mortgage broker and ask how much they could refinance for. And they did.

It turned out that an appraisal of their property valued it at $209,000. A 90 percent mortgage would give them a loan of $188,000, which, after costs, would net them $10,000 in cash. "It's like harvesting fruit from a tree," Leo said. You can refinance and then you'll be ready for your next property. He also pointed out that with really good credit, they could probably refinance for a higher LTV (loan-to-value), though that would mean bigger payments, which they did not want.

TIP

It's much easier to get cash out of a property on a refinance when you're an occupant-owner. Lenders don't like to give cash out on property that's rented.

"But," David pointed out, "we just getting a higher mortgage. If we buy another property, we'll need to get yet another mortgage. We'll have two. How can we make the payments?"

"By renting out one house," Leslie said. "We'll buy the next house the same way we bought this one. By moving in, we'll get the good owner-occupant financing, and we'll rent this old one out. We can keep playing the game over and over!"

"Yes, but won't the lenders get wise after a while? Can we just keep jumping from one property to the next, always claiming to be owner-occupants?"

Leo said that as long as they intended to occupy the property and acted on their intention, he didn't see any problem. If they lived in the property for a few years or so, he didn't see how anyone could question the fact that they bought with the intent of moving in.

"We can do one house every two years," Leslie quipped. "After 20 years, we'll own 10 houses, and half will be well on their way to being paid off!"

Leo smiled and said, "Many real estate fortunes have been built in just such a manner. And keep in mind that inflation and the national housing shortage will keep boosting those prices higher. Chances are that after 20 years, your first home will be worth two to three times what you originally paid for it!"

"Let's go!" David said, suddenly enthused.

TIP

It's called "serial investing," buying one house after another and then renting them out or selling them.

Learning to Flip

Leslie and David immediately began working on two fronts. First, they began looking for a tenant for their current home. At the same time they began looking for their next home investment.

As it turned out, David had several associates at work who were looking for new places to live. Two of them wanted to buy a home, and both were already preapproved, but a third, recently hired, wanted a rental. David told him that if he could hold on for a month or so until they found a new home, he could rent their old house. The associate said he'd try, but if something came along sooner, he'd take it. He was currently living in an apartment that was just too small for his family.

They also looked for new properties. During the year they had spent many weekends touring their area, going to "open houses" to get a sense of the market. Now they felt they had a good command of what prices should be and where to look. They were especially aware of homes in their tract. Which is how they came across the property on Morningstar Street.

It was just two blocks over from where they currently lived. The owners had bought it new. But they were now in the midst of a nasty divorce. They wanted to sell the property, fast.

Leslie happened to come by and was chatting with the wife, Sandy, in the front yard. Leslie said she was looking for a home to buy in the neighborhood, and Sandy explained about the divorce said she was anxious to sell. She asked if Leslie knew of anyone who wanted to buy it as a quick sale for $150,000, no commission. (It turned out they had paid only $135,000 for the property brand new years earlier.)

Leslie ran home and called Leo. She explained the situation, and Leo said that since she had found the seller and it wasn't listed, he would handle the deal for her for half a commission (which she would have to pay since the seller already said she wouldn't), which would amount to 3 percent. Leslie thought this was rather a lot since she, after all, had done the legwork and there was only the paperwork remaining. Leo said to think of it as the price of gaining experience. So she agreed.

Leo came over, and that night he and Leslie went to the Morningstar Street house. He presented an offer for $150,000 to Sandy and her husband, cash to the seller. Of course, Leslie and David would be getting new financing and putting only 3 percent down, as they had on their current home. Leo allowed only three weeks to close the deal since the sellers wanted out right away.

Assigning the Contract

David happened to mention to Leo that there were several coworkers looking for a home, and Leo asked if one of them might not be interested in the house. David said it was a possibility. So when Leo drew up the contract, after David's and Leslie's name, he wrote in "Or Assigns." What this means, said Leo, is that at your option (not the seller's) you can assign this contract to someone else.

Leslie wasn't sure what that meant. Leo explained that it simply meant that they could have someone else substitute for them as the buyer, perhaps one of David's coworkers. "Why don't you ask them if they're interested," Leo suggested. "Only tell them that the price is $200,000. That's still almost $10,000 below market."

David made a quick calculation. "If we buy for $150,000 and quickly sell for $200,000, we'll make $50,000 profit!"

Leo smiled and noted that there would be costs, including his commission, which would probably eat up about $10,000. But, there probably would be over $40,000 left. That was called "flipping" the property. (Check into Chapter 10 for the perils of flipping.)

David called his associates immediately, and one definitely was interested. She came over, and David arranged with the sellers for her to see the property. She liked it, and, after seeing what comps in the area were going for, she agreed to buy it for the $200,000 price. Since she and her husband were already preapproved, the financing was almost automatic, and they had the cash plus closing costs to put into purchasing the home.

David could hardly wait to call Leo. Leo said the deal sounded good but certain conditions had to be met on a sale like this. He explained that a big problem could arise if David and Leslie kept the true nature of the transaction a secret from the rebuyer (David's coworker). "If the rebuyer were to later discover that you had sold the home out of escrow for more than you paid for it, they might get mad and, ultimately, sue you—and me. Therefore, it's important that the rebuyers acknowledge, in writing, that they are aware of what's happening."

David was hesitant. "You mean you want me to tell my coworker that I'm paying $150,000 for a home she's buying for $200,000? She'll never go for it."

"Why not?" Leo countered. "She's getting it for almost $10,000 below market; she liked it at that price. What difference should it make to her what you paid for it?"

David reluctantly agreed that made sense. When David later explained the entire transaction to his coworker and said she had to sign a statement that she was aware of what David and Leslie were paying for the property, she had no objections. In fact, she looked upon David as a kind of real estate guru and wanted him to help her get started investing in real estate too!

"What about the sellers?" Leslie said. "We certainly won't tell them about what's happening, will we?"

"Certainly," said Leo. "While the sellers have already agreed to sell to you 'or assigns,' as a safety precaution it won't hurt to be sure they know what's happening, and agree to it in writing."

Leslie was hesitant. She said, "You want me to tell the sellers that we're going to resell the property out of escrow for $50,000 more than we're paying for it. They'll never agree."

"Why not?" asked Leo. "They've already signed a binding contract with you to sell the property at a price they were happy to receive. They agreed to allow you to assign it. Why should they object if you're going to resell it for a profit? They're getting what they wanted out of it."

Leslie was doubtful, but she agreed it made sense.

Leo had the escrow company handle all the paperwork. David's coworker approved a separate agreement with David for the higher $200,000 price. And escrow understood that when the sale was consummated, the title of the property would go to the coworker, not to David.

The coworker applied for and got financing on the Morningstar property. She put the down payment and closing costs into escrow. The sellers signed a deed. The title was cleared. And the sellers signed a statement that they were aware that the buyers were assigning the title to a second party and that the buyers (Leslie and David) were making a profit on the transaction.

Leslie said that Sandy, the seller whom she had originally talked to, signed the statement right away. But Sandy's husband didn't want to sign. He said they should wait. They could get much more money.

But Sandy pointed out that they had already agreed to the sale and getting out of it would be difficult, if not impossible. Further, even if they could, they would have to wait to get more. The bottom line was that they both wanted to get things over with, immediately. Leslie felt that both husband and wife wanted to get rid of the community property, finalize their divorce, and get on with their lives. Ultimately, for them the sale, even at $150,000, was a good thing.

TIP

Time is everything. If you can wait, you can get your price, eventually. If you have to sell right away, you'll only get what a fast buyer is willing to pay.

On the closing day, David's coworker's money was put into escrow (along with the new mortgage) and went to pay off the sellers, to Leo who got paid a $6,000 commission, and after some minor closing costs, to David and Leslie who got a check, at closing, for $43,000. Needless to say they were ecstatic!

"Let's go flip another!" David said.

Leo pointed out that the reason they were able to flip was because Leslie had found a property they could purchase at far below market price. "That doesn't happen every day," he said. "You have to be ready to take advantage of it when it does happen. But, otherwise, you have to plan on going forward with your investing in the traditional way, just as before. And by the way," Leo added, "don't forget to tell your accountant about your profit. You'll have taxes to pay on it."

TRAP

In some areas of the country, flipping using an assignment may not work (check with a good local agent or attorney). If it doesn't, then David and Leslie could have obtained an "option" to purchase the property. They could have then found the buyer, David's coworker, and handled the transaction in a fashion similar to that described above, exercising their option when escrow closed.

Moving on to a Fixer-Upper

"If we can't find another property to flip, then where else can we multiply our profits?" David asked.

Leo suggested, "You might try a fixer-upper. I was hesitant to suggest it until you got your feet wet, but now that you have some experience, it might be just the thing to try."

Leo explained that a fixer-upper (called a "handyman special" in some parts of the country) is a distressed home. It might just need paint and cosmetic work. Or there might be something seriously wrong with it such as a cracked foundation or leaking roof. Or it might even be damaged to the extent that it's financially unsalvageable. "When it costs more to fix up the house than to bulldoze it and start over, it's called a 'scraper.' You just scrape it off the lot and start again. That's usually the domain of contractors and builders. A fixer-upper is a salvageable house"

Leo suggested that they hunt for homes that were the least distressed, needing only paint and minor cosmetic repairs. David and Leslie agreed.

They spent several weekends going through the Multiple Listing Service (MLS) books checking out those properties listed by agents that had descriptions such as "Needs TLC" or "Just waiting for a handy owner." Many were, indeed, in run-down condition. However, they found that almost always, the sellers were asking very close to market price for the home, as if it were in good condition. The sellers weren't discounting the properties because of their distressed condition. "Most sellers refuse to acknowledge that their property is worth less when it's run down. They still want top dollar. They just sit on it and wonder why it doesn't sell. Finding a realistic seller is what makes locating a good fixer-upper so difficult."

After they had checked out and dismissed everything that was currently in the MLS, Leslie took to driving through neighborhoods nearby their home. She would stop at *for-sale-by-owner homes* (FSBOs) in the hope that some of these would be suitable.

Many of these qualified as distressed properties. But FSBO sellers seemed to ask even more than sellers of listed properties. The sellers seemed to think that because they were selling the property without an agent that the buyer should pay as much—and sometimes more—as he or she would pay for a property listed with an agent. Leo pointed out that 85 percent of all FSBO sellers eventually gave up and listed their home with agents. The most common reason the FSBO sellers weren't able to sell their home was that they had overpriced it for the market.

One day Leslie came across a home that looked very distressed, but it had no for-sale sign on it. The lawn hadn't been mowed lately, and weeds were sprouting everywhere. A screen on one front window was torn and hanging loose, and even the front door looked shabby. She stopped and knocked, but no one was home. So she wrote a note on a three- by five-inch card saying she was interested in buying a home such as this one, and in the note she included her phone number. She slid the note under the front door and left.

TIP

Real estate agents "farm" areas for listings. That means they cover a neighborhood, or group of neighborhoods, knocking on doors and talking to people hoping to discover someone who will want to sell. By sticking to one area and repeating their efforts, they become known and frequently get new listings. There's no reason that you, an investor, can't do the same thing when you want to find good investment property.

That night Leslie got a call from Gloria who said she had found Leslie's card and indeed she did want to sell her home. But it was in foreclosure. Could Leslie stop by to talk it over? Leslie agreed to do so.

The next day Leslie and Leo went to see Gloria and hear her story. Gloria and her husband had bought the home seven years earlier. They had made all the payments until her husband lost his job eight months earlier. Neither he nor she had been able to find steady work, and they had fallen behind. Now they were nearly five months in arrears in their payments, and the mortgage lender had sent them a "notice of default" and had begun foreclosure proceedings.

Leo explained that in California, as in most but not all states, a *deed of trust* is used by lenders. That allows foreclosure without going to court. In California, after a notice of default is filed, the borrower (called the *trustor*) has 90 days to pay up all the back payments on the mortgage plus additional penalties, interest, and costs. If the borrower does not pay up in that time, the lender (called the *beneficiary*) "gives notice" to the trustee (who actually holds the title to the property—typically a title insurance company) by advertising in a local paper that the trustee will be selling the home "on the courthouse steps" after two weeks. The "two weeks" are the *borrower's period of redemption*. In Gloria and her husband's case, this provision meant that they could redeem the property by paying off the mortgage in full (as opposed to making up back payments and costs). If they were not able to redeem the property during that period, it would be sold to the highest bidder, and Gloria and husband would no longer have any interest in it.

TIP

Each state has its own procedures and time limits for foreclosure. If you're interested in working foreclosures, you should check with a good attorney or agent in your state to find out how it's carried out there. You may also want to read my book, *Finding Hidden Real Estate Bargains*, McGraw-Hill, 2nd edition, 2002.

Gloria explained that it had been eleven weeks since they had received their notice of default, so they had only a few weeks left to do something before the property was lost. Gloria asked if Leslie would buy it. She said she would *if* she could get it for little enough to pay for fixing it up and making a profit. Leo added that if they wanted his services, there would also, of course, be his commission.

Later that day, David came over, and he and Leslie made a list of all the things necessary to restore the house to good condition. Then they secured estimates of how much it would cost to do these. Their list included the following:

NEEDED TO FIX-UP THE HOUSE ON DIAMOND STREET

1. Paint inside and out. -	$5,000
2. Replace fixtures in one bathroom and kitchen sink and counter top. -	$2,500
3. Repair doors, windows, screens, and two broken walls.	$1,500
4. Replace wall-to-wall carpeting. -	$4,500
5. Restore landscaping. -	$1,200
Total	$14,700

"Don't forget the real estate agent's commission," David said.

Leslie replied that she didn't see any need for a hiring an agent since she had done all the work herself. Besides, they now had experience in handling deals. She said they should go it alone.

David wasn't so sure. "Why not ask Leo if he will just advise us for, say, $1,000?"

When Leslie called Leo and passed along David's suggestion, Leo said he was a full-service agent who didn't sell his services on a fee basis. The liability was the same whether he got a full commission or just a grand, so he'd do it only for the full commission. However, he understood why they wanted to go it alone, and he wished them well. He hoped they would think of him after they had fixed up the property and would consider listing then. Leslie said they certainly would.

TIP

Fee-for-service and discount brokers are popping up all over the country. Today many agents will handle just the paperwork or some other aspect of a transaction for a set fee.

Leo then gave them some free advice. He suggested that they be sure to get title insurance on the property. Otherwise, they might end up owning a home with hidden mortgages or other liens on it.

Leslie thanked him. Then she and Gloria worked out a deal.

Buying the Foreclosure on Diamond Street

Leslie put it all down on paper so they both could see.

Fix-up work: Leslie said it would cost $15,000 to restore the house to good condition:	$15,000
Remedy foreclosure: Gloria brought out all the paperwork, and Leslie and she discovered that in addition to paying off the mortgage (it would soon be in the redemption phase when the lender would no longer accept back payments and so on but would demand a full payoff), it would cost an additional $8,000 in back interest and penalties plus the mortgage amount, or $168,000.	$168,000
Resale costs: In addition, when David and Leslie resold the home, there would be other costs, perhaps another $10,000 including at least a partial commission to a real estate agent:	$10,000
Profit: Finally, Leslie said it wouldn't be worth David's and her time and risk unless she could make at least $25,000 profit on the deal.	$25,000
Total:	$218,000

The next question became, how much would the house actually be worth on the market, after it was fixed up? If it wasn't worth at least $218,000, then the deal wouldn't make sense.

Leslie secured a comparative market analysis (CMA) with which she determined that the home would be worth about $240,000 on the market after it had been restored to good condition. So it was actually worth $22,000 more!

Leslie said that this money represented the remains of Gloria's equity and would go to her and her husband.

Gloria called her husband in and explained the deal. He was adamantly opposed. He asked why they should take $22,000 for what was in reality a much bigger equity.

Leslie explained that their equity really wasn't bigger at all. No matter who bought the home, chances are it would cost a lot to put it in shape and resell it (in her case $15,000 to fix it up, $168,000 to pay off the loan, $10,000 to resell, and $25,000 to include her profit).

Gloria added that they were going to lose the place within a few weeks unless they acted right away, and if they lost it, they'd have nothing. Leslie reminded him that the home was a wreck. She was assuming risk in buying it because of all the work that had to be done. If she couldn't get the work done at the prices she had been quoted and resell the house at full market price, she might be in their shoes in just a few months.

Gloria's husband then reluctantly agreed. He said that asking $25,000 profit didn't seem so terrible from that perspective. Both Gloria and her husband signed a sales agreement that Leslie had a local attorney prepare.

TIP

Attorneys, particularly on the East Coast, will often handle all the paperwork for a real estate transaction for a fee between $500 and $1,500—probably the biggest bargain in legal work today!

TRAP

Many states, including California, have laws that regulate the purchase of a home that's in foreclosure. Some of these may offer the seller a chance to redeem the home at a later date, even after you've done all the work fixing it up! In other cases, you may need to offer the sellers a five-day opportunity to back out of the deals. Check with a good local agent or attorney for such potential pitfalls when purchasing foreclosures in your area.

Then it was just a matter of beating the clock.

Leslie and David opened escrow and contacted their mortgage broker, who said he could get them a $192,000 mortgage. That meant the loan would be for 80 percent of the home's value, called the *loan-to-value* (LTV). However, the lender insisted on a 10 percent *holdback* because of the property's condition. The holdback meant that 10 percent of the mortgage would be held back by the lender until the home was refurbished to ensure that the work was actually completed. So on closing, they'd only get 70 percent ($173,000). They would receive the additional 10 percent ($19,000) later.

David asked about the closing costs for obtaining the loan. The lender explained that in this situation, the costs for acquiring the mortgage would be built into the interest rate and that the interest rate would therefore be 3/8 percent higher than it would have been if they had paid the closing costs in cash.

TIP

Mortgage costs can be paid in three ways: The borrower can pay the costs in cash up front, the lender can build the costs into the mortgage by raising the mortgage amount, or the lender can build the costs into the interest charges by writing the mortgage at a higher interest rate.

To make the deal, Leslie and David had to put an additional $19,000 of their own money (profit from their Morningstar property) into escrow. Of course, as soon as they were finished fixing up the property, the remainder of the mortgage ($19,000) would be paid to them, meaning they had purchased the property for virtually nothing except the fixing-up costs.

CLOSING THE DIAMOND STREET HOME

From the new mortgage		$173,000
From David and Leslie		19,000
To pay-off old mortgage	$168,000	
To pay-off Gloria	22,000	
Escrow and title ins. fees	2,000	
	$192,000	192,000

They now owned the property on Diamond Street. And they set about fixing it up.

Fixing up Diamond Street

David and Leslie began fixing up the property as soon as they got possession of it. The first thing they did was work on the landscaping since it would take the longest to handle. David put in a new lawn in front while Leslie planted flowers and shrubs in front and on the sides.

Then they replaced and repaired sinks, doors, cabinets, countertops, and windows. When everything was in tip-top shape, they had the home painted inside and out. Finally, they put in new wall-to-wall carpeting.

When they looked at their bills, they found it had cost them $20,000 to fix up the house, plus another $2,000 to pay the carrying costs for the mortgage, taxes, and insurance during the six weeks of work. They had budgeted only $15,000, which meant that the extra $7,000 would come out of their profit.

TRAP

It's vitally important to use a very sharp pencil when calculating fix-up costs. Every dollar you are off eventually means that much money out of your pocket.

While David was very upset about that, Leslie pointed out an unexpected bonus. The house looked terrific! "Instead of reselling it right away, let's move in," She suggested.

"But what about the house on Horizon Drive?" David asked.

"We'll rent it," she replied. "Isn't that what we intended to do anyway? Besides, even with the extra costs, we're still ahead with the money we made flipping Morningstar Street."

So they moved out of their first investment house and into their fixer-upper. (Once moved in, they could refinance as owner-occupants and get their fixing-up money out too.)

Renting out Horizon Drive

Now they were becoming landlords. Their next task was renting out the Horizon Drive property. David immediately contacted the coworker who had said he was interested in finding a rental, but David discovered that the man had already rented elsewhere. So they put an ad in the local paper.

The ad was small, just giving the size, amenities, and rental rate. They had confirmed a rate that was appropriate for the area by checking again with other landlords who were advertising rentals. They knew their rate was $50 below market.

They received many calls and frequently showed the property. They had their attorney prepare a month-to-month contract as well as a would-be tenant application.

TRAP

Beware of rental applications and contracts that you can buy in stationery stores. Often they do not contain enough "boilerplate" language to protect your interests. For more information on rental agreements, check into my book *The Landlord's Trouble Shooter*, 2/e, Dearborn, $17.95.

They had each serious prospective tenant fill out an application, which gave them permission to call the applicant's previous landlords as well as get a credit report. Eventually, they narrowed their prospects down to a couple with two children who had excellent credit as well as excellent recommendations from their two previous landlords. They rented on a month-to-month basis, for which they were very glad later on.

TIP

Month-to-month means that either party can break the rental agreement with 30 days' notice. This type of contract gives both parties much more flexibility than a long-term lease.

Selling a Property

When another year had gone by, Leslie said, "It's time. Let's get another property. Only, let's sell our first home on Horizon Drive first and get our cash out. There are a lot of things I'd like to buy." David nodded. It was so easy to please Leslie. Besides, some of the money could be used on a new sports car.

They called Leo and said they wanted to list their first property on Horizon Drive. Leo came by, and they talked for a while, and then Leo said, "Selling isn't a good idea. You've rented it out for a year. It's now a property held for investment. If you sell outright, you'll have to pay taxes on your gain."

Leslie and David nodded. They expected to pay taxes.

"In real estate," Leo continued, "investors abhor paying taxes on their gains, particularly when there's a way to legally avoid it. If you want to get out of your Horizon Drive property, then why not trade for another?"

"Trade?" both Leslie and David asked.

"Yes," Leo replied. "You're going to invest your money in another property anyhow, aren't you?"

They both nodded.

"Okay, then," Leo said. "Instead of selling and then buying, why not just trade for that next property? In so doing, you can defer paying taxes and instead switch your tax liability from the old property to the new. You can use all of your equity to buy the next property instead of losing part of it to pay taxes. You'll end up with a bigger property!"

TRAP

Real estate taxation is a separate and complex subject. Before making any moves that would affect your tax situation, you should see a good accountant or tax attorney.

David and Leslie listened closely. Leo explained that the most common way for investors to defer (or put off) the payment of gain with investment real estate was to use a *1031 tax-deferred exchange.* "It's not really that complicated, but it has some strict rules. Basically this type of transaction means that you take the profit from this house and put it into another like-kind property. You don't take any money out. You switch."

David asked about, "*Like-kind?*" Leo explained it was a technical term that referred to the property type. It doesn't mean you have to trade a house for a house. It means you have to trade property held for business or investment for other property held for business or investment. It could be a duplex for a house, for example.

"But," Leslie said, "we can't take any money out? David wants to buy a new car."

"No," Leo continued., "That's one of the rules. There can be no 'boot' or cash-out as part of the deal, else it will be nullified and you'll owe taxes. Of course, you could refinance either before the transaction or the next house after if you needed cash.

TRAP

A "Starker" IRS code 1031(a)(3) tax-deferred exchange has other important rules including strict timelines that must be adhered to. See below and Chapter 12 for more details.

"Trading sounds okay," said Leslie, "but, I want another house we can move into. If we have to trade for a like-kind, that means the new property will have to be a rental too, doesn't it?"

Leo nodded, "You might lose the tax-deferred status of the deal if you immediately moved into the new home." When they both looked crestfallen, he said, "I have an alternative plan. Why not move back into your Horizon Drive home and live there for a while? Then sell it as your personal residence. Then when you sell, chances are you won't have any taxes at all to pay."

Converting to a Rental and Back

Both Leslie and David leaned forward to make sure they had heard correctly. "Move back in. No taxes on our profit?"

"None at all," Leo said. "The federal government has a $250,000 exclusion ($500,000 per married couple) when you sell your personal residence, provided you meet the qualifications. If you do, then any gain up to those levels is tax free. You can take the money and do with it as you will."

"What are the qualifications?" David asked carefully.

Leo explained that basically there were two: "One, you must have lived in the property for the previous two out of five years. You already lived there for over a year before you rented it out. Move back in and live there another year, and you will have fulfilled the two-out-of-the-five requirement. (You can only sell and claim the exemption once every two years.)"

"But," David countered, "we won't have lived there for two consecutive years."

"Doesn't matter," Leo said. "Any combination of two out of five will do, even if it's measured by months."

Leo went on, "The second qualification is that the home must be your principal residence. In other words, it must be your main home, where you reside most of the time. The problem in your present situation is that you converted the Horizon Avenue property to a rental so now it's investment property. In order for it to be your principal residence, you have to move back in."

"That's it?" David asked. "So, we have to move back to the Horizon Avenue house and live in it for another year?"

"Yes," Leo replied.

TIP

You don't have to be living in the property when you sell it. You just have to have lived in it for the previous two out of five years. It could currently be a rental, provided that you have met the two-out-of-five requirement.

"And that's it?" Leslie asked.

"That's basically it," Leo said. "You can do it as many times as you like. There's no limit, as long as it's no more than once every two years." He pointed out there were a number of other concerns, and told them to check with their accountant for the details, and they did.

David and Leslie gave their tenants one month's notice. The tenants were upset because they had anticipated living in the home for a longer time period. So Leslie and David asked if they'd like to switch and live in their fixer-upper on Diamond Street (from which David and Leslie were moving). It was only a few miles away, and it was in great shape. (The tenants had proved to be excellent by paying their rent on time and keeping the property tidy, so switching would be perfect for Leslie and David.)

The rents were not much different, and the Diamond Street house was nicer, so the tenants agreed, and they swapped.

TIP

Manipulating tenants can be difficult. Often when they are forced to move out, they will choose to look for another rental that's bigger, cheaper, closer to work, or something similar. Don't count on being able to "switch" tenants very often.

Qualifying for the Exclusion

Leslie and David lived in the Horizon Drive home for another year. They had previously lived in it for a year before moving into the Diamond Street rental, so after two years they felt they had qualified for the up to $500,000 per couple exclusion.

Six weeks before the two years were up, they called Leo and said they wanted to list the property. He happily took their listing explaining that prices had gone up considerably. Their home was now worth $250,000, which they already knew having run a CMA through the Web.

They had discussed selling the home as a FSBO without using Leo as an agent, but they decided that they really didn't want to take the time off from work to do it. Besides, in order to sell it as a FSBO, they might have had to lower the price below market to attract a buyer. So the buyer would have ended up benefiting more from their house selling as a FSBO than they would. "Chances are we'd net almost as much paying a commission as we would by cutting the price to the level of a FSBO," Leslie said. Then there was the time it would take to sell. Besides, they felt they owed one to Leo.

The home sold within a month for nearly full market price, $245,000. At the close of escrow they netted roughly $50,000, tax free.

Profit on Horizon Drive

Sales price	$245,000	
First mortgage		$170,000
Second mortgage		6,000
Commission		15,000
Closing costs		2,000
	193,000	193,000
Profit	$52,000	

"Now we have to find another place to live!" said Leslie.

Leslie and David went on to buy other investment homes. *Their next venture was to trade the fixer-upper on Diamond Street for a fourplex*, a small apartment building with four large units. They did a 1031 tax-deferred exchange under the guidance of Leo and their accountant. As part of the sale they made sure that they abided by at least the following stipulations.

Making a 1031 Tax-Deferred Trade

1. They identified the new property within 45 days after (or prior to) the sale.

2. They closed on the new property within 180 days.

3. There was no "boot" or cash-out to them.

4. The new property was of "like-kind."

They also fulfilled several other requirements that their accountant insisted upon. For more information on trading properties, see Chapter 12 in this book and my book *Buy, Rent, and Sell,* McGraw-Hill, 2001.

Moving On

The last I heard of Leslie and David, they were continuing to buy homes to live in and invest in. They continued to trade up investment properties and were soon buying apartment houses and "strip" shopping malls. And every two years they sold their principal residence, in which they were living, and collected the profit tax free.

Of course, one wonders what they'll do once their profits exceed the exclusion limit of $500,000, but that's a big figure still a ways off, and their accountant says she'll come up with something else by then!

2
The Hidden Rules Of Successful Real Estate Investing

You want to get started investing in real estate, but you're just not sure what you need. How much money does it take? What sort of financial condition do you need to be in? What should be your goals? What's a realistic time frame? Is a particular mindset useful or even necessary?

These are reasonable questions to ask. After all, you don't want to dive into a pool until you've determined how deep the water is. Similarly, you shouldn't dive into real estate investing until you've plumbed the financial depths involved.

In this chapter we'll answer these and other questions that first-time investors are likely to have.

How Much Money Do I Need?

As we saw in the last chapter, not a whole lot. Of course, the amount depends on where you're starting. If you want to buy your first rental house, and *if* you're willing to move into it for a while (as Leslie and David did) before you subsequently rent it out and resell it, then the very best financing in the world is available to you.

You can get a mortgage for as much as 103 percent of the purchase price. That means you can get financing to cover *all* of the cost of the home plus virtually *all* of the cost of the closing. Your out-of-pocket expenses are zero. Where else can you get into an investment for as little?! (In Chapter 13 we'll go into the details of financing.)

Of course, it's a different story if you buy a home with the express intention of using it as an investment rental. You'll need to put about 10 percent down plus closing costs. On a $200,000 home, that's about $25,000— a substantial sum of money.

Should I Invest Full-Time?

In the beginning it's usually a mistake to invest in real estate as a full-time job. For most people the best way to invest in property is usually on a part-time basis. It's important to understand that initially it's unlikely that you'll get enough income to live on out of your properties. After a few years, when the properties have aged, and values and rental rates have gone up, it's a different story. But for the first 10 years, it's better to think in terms of reinvesting, rather than withdrawing, income.

TRAP

Be very wary of so-called real estate gurus who promise you tens of thousands of dollars of annual income from real estate from the moment you begin investing. If it is that easy, why aren't they making millions doing it themselves instead of selling get-rich-quick seminars on the subject. (By the way—in case you haven't already guessed—this is *not* a get-rich-quick book. Here we're talking about building your wealth in real estate the proven old-fashioned way—over time.)

All of which is to say that you need to have a steady full-time job for at least the first 10 years you are investing because your property won't likely yield enough steady income for you to live on. The most successful real estate investors I've known (your author included) buy property for the long term. If you go the long-term route, you won't have to worry as much about making occasional mistakes— because property values almost always go up with inflation and housing shortages, so eventually you'll come out all right.

Aiming at first just to break even, most investors don't count on taking money out monthly. After a few years, however, when rental rates go up, they will probably be able to take out a strong, steady stream of income.

So consider investing in real estate on the side. For a while at least, don't make it your primary objective.

In other words, don't quit your day job! Just keep at it for enough years, and you'll be able to retire early with a huge bounty to rely on.

TIP

Make your goal part-time investing in real estate.

How Quickly Can I Get My Money Out of Real Estate Investments If I Need To?

You should plan on holding real estate investments for the long term because you're building your net worth (the more properties you own, presumably the greater your wealth over time) and also because this wealth tends to be illiquid.

In the span of a few years you might easily acquire a million dollars or more in equity in property. But you'll probably have very little cash in the bank. (This situation is spoken of as being "cash poor," a common condition for real estate investors.)

Being cash poor, however, is no longer the serious problem it was in the past. Today, with equity loans and all types of refinancing possible, it's much easier to get cash out of your investment properties when you need it. All of which is to say that if you own a lot of property and have a sudden big personal expense, you'll probably have the means to easily cover it.

For example, let's say a big personal expense comes up such as a sudden illness, a wedding, college education, or the need for a new car—anything that requires a lot of money. To get the money you need, you can refinance a property. (Alternatively, you could also sell a property, but that could take more time and you would no longer have your investment.)

I always cringe when I hear those who purport to be financial advisors advise young couples to put away a certain percentage of their income (usually into stocks and bonds, which these advisors often just happen to be selling) so that the couple will have the money to pay for their children's college education and their own retirement. (This philosophy seems to be that you should live less well today by scrimping and saving so that you can live less well tomorrow!)

How much better it is to own a bunch of homes and other real estate, nearly paid off, that you can harvest for the money you need for these expenses when you need it. And you don't have to be scrimping and saving your entire life to pay for these expenses—your tenants will handle that for you!

TIP

Your goal: Acquire properties in order to have the money you need for life's big expenses.

What's My Time Frame?

Or, how long will it take to make my fortune in real estate? Of course, we've touched on this in many places. The answer is, figure on as much as 10 years or more, and 20 years is ideal.

Yes, you may be very lucky and come across a series of properties that you can flip, split (subdivide one property into two, thus doubling your money), or otherwise sell for a big profit. But depending on that is like gambling on the lottery. It's great if it comes in, but don't count on it. Instead, rely on the slow and steady and sure.

Think of it in simple terms. As our couple, Leslie and David, did in the first chapter, plan on buying one house every year or two for 20 years. At the end of that time you'll own 10 to 20 houses. The first house will be roughly half paid off. (The return on equity from a mortgage is the greatest in the last years, the least in the first years. Thus after paying two-thirds of the time on the mortgage, the house will be roughly only half paid off.) Further, inflation and housing shortages likely will make that first house worth two to three times what you paid for it, *no matter what you paid for it!*

Chances are that by the end of that 20-year period, you'll have a million dollars or more in equity that you can convert to cash if you need to. In addition, you'll have positive cash flow as well. Remember, rental rates on those early properties will go up (because of inflation and national housing shortages in many areas) just as prices do. You'll be renting them for two to three times the original rent even though your mortgage payments will be roughly the same as when you started (assuming you haven't refinanced)!

All of which is to say that in addition to having a large net worth, you'll also have a large monthly income, over time. This is the point at which you can retire from your regular job and live off your properties.

And remember, we're not talking about doing something difficult or arcane. We're talking about buying one property every year or two for 20 years. What could be simpler?!

Of course, there may be obstacles. You could have a bad year and lose your job for a time. But even if that happens, while you might not be able to buy a new home that year, you'll have the homes you already own to fall back upon.

TIP

Your goal: Aim for a timeline of 10 to 20 years.

Of course, those who see the glass as always half empty will say you could get sick, or die, or the economy could nosedive. Yes, those things could happen. But they're going to happen whether or not you invest in real estate. So why not invest and hope for the best?

What Mindset Do I Need to Be a Successful Investor?

There is really only one requirement—that you understand the difference between your business and your personal life.

When buying a home for investment, you will feel countless tugs, against your better judgment, to buy a property because it offers so many pleasing features. You may love the layout of the kitchen. The tile in the bathroom can be adorable. The backyard may be perfect for your family. The garage is ideal because it's big with lots of storage space—and there's a workbench!

All of the above would be good reasons to select a home for your personal life, a home that would be most suited to your tastes, needs, and desires. However, when buying investment property, you need to put all that aside and let the reasoning portion of your mind take over. You need to be all business.

The questions to ask are: Will this feature or that one be suitable for tenants? Is it easily replaced if it is damaged or destroyed? Will the feature make the house more or less saleable in the future? You have to put aside all personal feelings when you consider the property. You must be strictly business.

This also applies when it comes to money. When it's time to buy or sell a property, you must go for the very best deal possible. You can't let yourself be swayed by feeling sorry for the other party's situation. For example, tenants may tell you they can't (or won't) pay their rent because they have so many other bills. You have to be strong enough to tell them, "The rent comes first," and demand immediate payment. (If you acquiesce to a tenant's problem, it then becomes your problem because you don't have the rental money with which to pay your bills.)

Similarly when negotiating for the purchase or sale of a home, you may find you're dealing with people who have all sorts of personal problems from illness, to divorce, to bankruptcy. Your heart may go out to them. However, the way you help them is not to make their problem yours (by paying too much or selling for too little). It's by removing a problem from them. For example, you can help a person who is destined to lose his or her house to foreclosure by buying it from them, which will help to save their credit. If you want to go further and give them money to get them back on their feet, I applaud you. However, be sure you understand your motivation. Getting their home out of foreclosure was business. Helping them is charity. Both are admirable, but it's important not to confuse one with the other.

What Other Qualities Do I Need to Be Successful?

I have been asked if a successful real estate investor needs to have a mind that pays attention to detail. The answer is yes, certainly. But then again, it's hard to imagine any line of endeavor where lack of attention to detail is an asset. You'll find that you need to keep track of market values, rental payments, and all sorts of numbers. A good ledger (or Palm Pilot) will help. But it's still up to you to remember the details.

I have also been asked if a person needs to be a "people person" to make a good real estate investor. Again, it's hard to imagine any line of work where personal interactions aren't important. However, in real estate *investing*, they can be less important than elsewhere.

You don't need to "sell yourself" to purchase investment property or to be a landlord. Although a pleasing personality and a determination to deal fairly with people are great assets here and elsewhere in this business, many very successful real estate investors are reclusive. You almost never see them and when you do, they don't have 10 words to say. On the other hand, if you intend to sell a property on your own (FSBO), then it helps to be gregarious in nature. You'll be dealing directly with potential buyers, and if you have an ability to chat and make friends easily, it will help. Of course, you don't have to sell FSBO because you can always sell through an agent.

Thus, it turns out that you don't need a lot of money to get started. But you do need determination and the ability to separate your business from your personal life. You also need to understand that you're in it for the long term, so, as I said, don't quit your day job, at least not right away.

3

Finding Good Investment Properties

There are over 65 million homes in the United States, and the vast majority are single-family dwellings. For the beginning investor, this inventory represents a huge treasure-trove of getting-started properties. They are everywhere. To find the best one for you, you just have to know how to sift through the pile.

Before jumping in, however, it's important to clearly define what we're looking for. As we saw in the first chapter, a house makes a great first investment, probably the best. However, it's not just any house we want—it's a house we can make a profit on. That means that we must be able to buy it inexpensively. The ideal investment property will sell for below market price. Where do we find it?

In this chapter we're going to consider five areas:

1. Properties listed with local agents
2. Properties listed as "for sale by owner" (FSBOs)
3. Properties listed on the Internet
4. Foreclosures and properties listed as "real estate owned" (REOs)
5. Government repos

Work the Listings

In any endeavor, it's important to take advantage of what's already out there to help you. In other words, if you want to build a wheelbarrow, it's wise not to set about reinventing the wheel.

Already in place is a vast network of listed properties. Indeed, at any given time, probably around 85 percent of the properties for sale are listed with agents. So the first step is to tap into this resource.

TIP

As a buyer, unless you're using a buyer's broker (discussed in Chapter 5), you probably won't have to pay a commission on your purchase—that's the seller's problem. So, if you find a good one, why not buy a listed property?

I've heard many beginning investors say something like, "There's nothing good listed. If there were, an investor or agent would have already bought it!" That's a mistake in thinking. Normally there are so many properties for sale at any given time that there are bargains out there just waiting to be discovered. Further, every agent I've ever known would much rather get a commission, which means immediate income, than buy a listed property, which means a long-term investment. Agents need that constant influx of cash that commissions supply to survive. Normally, they buy for investment only as a last resort.

All of which is to say that the person who complains about the lack of bargains in listings probably hasn't taken the time to look. Only after you've spent a month or two checking out all currently listed properties in your area should you conclude that there's nothing for you in the MLS.

Contact an Agent

You'll want to work with an agent who has access to the Multiple Listing Service (MLS) in your area. Agents who have MLS access are usually members of the National Association of Realtors(NAR). Also check into Chapter 5 for more information on working with agents.

Tell your agent exactly what you're interested in. If you're just getting started, like Leslie and David in the first chapter, chances are you're looking for a house both as a place to live and as an investment. You have your choice of the greatest selection of properties on the MLS.

Keeping in mind the criteria for an investment/live in property that we went into detail on in Chapter 1, now look for the bargain, or those which the sellers have indicated they are willing to negotiate on.

TIP

Here are nine tips for buying good investment/live in homes:

1. Buy close to where you live and/or work.
2. Look for good schools.
3. Check for pride-of-ownership in the neighborhood.
4. Aim for a neighborhood with a low crime rate.
5. Look for a neighborhood close to shopping and transportation access.
6. Get the minimum size that will appeal to renters.
7. Look for an area with a good supply of tenants.
8. Look for a property that will be suitable for renting.
9. Look for a property that can be easily maintained.

Look for Stale Listings

Stale properties are those that have been listed the longest. A seller who puts a property on the market on Monday isn't likely to cut his or her price by Friday. On the other hand, a seller who's had his or her property on the market for three months with no activity is likely to be very anxious to make a deal—and cut his or her price to do it.

TIP

A typical listing contract is written for 90 days. At the end of that time, the agent is more likely to put pressure on the seller to accept any offer. After all, if the seller decides not to renew the contract after 90 days, the agent will lose the listing—and a commission.

In a normal market, a large number of properties will be in the stale category. Indeed, most properties will take two months or more to sell. In a slow market, you'll want to extend your time frame to homes that have gone unsold for six months or longer. In a hot market, however, you will have to reduce that time frame, sometimes to a few weeks.

Look for Price Reductions

Another indication that a seller is anxious to dump a property is a price reduction, particularly a large reduction. A seller who cuts the price by $1,000 is merely trying to attract attention. A seller who cuts the price by $10,000 is serious.

Multiple price reductions—particularly when they come in close succession—indicate a very anxious seller. I once bought a home from sellers who were so anxious to sell that they were cutting their price $10,000 a week until they finally sold the property. If I had waited long enough, I could have gotten the property for nothing!—although certainly someone else would have bought it long before then.

When you find a property that has been reduced in price and that otherwise seems suitable (see the rules above), don't feel you have to offer the current asking price. Just because a seller has reduced the price doesn't mean the price is at rock bottom. Treat a reduced price as you would any other—the starting point for negotiations. Work down from there.

Check for Clues in the Listings

Listing agents have a duty to protect their clients, in this case, the sellers, and they must do everything they can to attract buyers. This means letting buyers know when sellers are highly motivated to sell, which they accomplish often by writing clues into the listing.

Look for phrases such as "highly motivated" or "bring in all offers" or "wants to move immediately." You get the idea: The agent is sending out the word that this seller is very anxious and will consider low-ball offers. If the property is also listed with price reductions, you probably have a real opportunity in the making.

Check Out the Properties

While this may seem simple minded, the fact is that some beginning investors prefer the paperwork to the legwork. They will find a property that looks terrific on paper and make an offer.

Another mistake: Real estate properties are not homogenous. That means that every property has unique characteristics. No matter how good a property looks on paper, you have to check it out physically before you make on offer for it. You might find that this terrific property backs up to a dump site. Or it has high-tension electric wires traveling over the fence line. Or the street in front is all broken up and the city has no plans to fix it. Or . . . Nothing takes the place of looking at a property.

Work the For-Sale-By-Owner Properties (FSBOs)

Not all properties are listed. Some are being sold by their owners direct to sellers. When they see such listings, many beginning investors immediately jump to the conclusion that because there is no agent's commission involved, these listings must be bargains. Beware: In most cases these are far from bargains. What you're looking for are the occasional FSBOs that can make you a profit.

TIP

Most FSBO sellers plan on pocketing the money they expect to save by not going through an agent. The last thing in their minds is giving it to you, the investment buyer. Therefore, you need to find that rare FSBO seller who has common sense, who will give you the money saved in order to get a quick sale.

Drive through Neighborhoods with Investment Potential

While FSBOs are advertised, really the best way to find the ones that would work for you is to drive through the neighborhoods in which you're interested. Remember, we discussed the advantages of buying a property in an area close to where you work. Think of this area as your "farm." You'll define certain neighborhoods as good investment areas and, on a fairly regular basis, drive or walk through them. Look for signs that indicate a person is selling his or her home FSBO.

When you find an FSBO that looks suitable, based on the criteria at the beginning of this chapter, stop by and engage the seller-owner in discussion. Find out what the asking price is and if there are any special features. Then check it out—do a comparative market analysis (CMA). Chances are you'll find that the FSBO price is at, or maybe even higher than, market price!

How can a seller even think that, you may be asking yourself? Why would I want to spend as much on a property without the benefit of an agent as I would with an agent? The reason the price is so high is that, quite frankly, most FSBO sellers don't think about the work involved in selling their property as much as they do about saving a big commission. Hence, they price their homes unrealistically.

Look for the Lone FSBO Seller Who Is Realistic

You will occasionally find an FSBO seller who sees the light. He or she has priced his or her home *below* market in order to attract buyers. Rather than attempt to save a commission, this seller will give the commission to the buyer (in the form of a lower price) in order to get a faster sale. This is someone with whom you can reason—and negotiate.

This is not to say that you should immediately pay the full asking price, even if it is below market. You should still negotiate, even lowball. But, it's much better to start with a realistic seller than with a seller who thinks his or her property is so wonderful that you ought to pay full price for it.

Keep in mind, however, that buying FSBO is more difficult. You don't have an agent to handle the paperwork and other details. Many investment buyers in this situation will find it advisable to hire a fee-for-service attorney or agent to handle the paperwork for them. It probably will only cost around $1,000, and, if you're new to real estate investing, it can be well worth the money.

Check Out the Internet

Today, virtually every property that's listed with an agent or that is being sold FSBO is also listed somewhere on the Internet. Listed property can be found on sites such as www.realtor.com (operated in cooperation with the NAR—National Association of Realtors) or *www.cyberhomes.com.*

FSBO sites come and go. Rather than list any here, your best bet is to check out one of the search engines such as YAHOO or MSN and simply write in the keyword FSBO in their search engine. You'll immediately be given dozens of suggestions which offer listings from direct sellers.

Pros and Cons of Working the Internet

Before beginning, it's important to understand the limitations as well as the advantages of searching for bargain properties on the Web. The advantages include the following:

- Easily viewed listings of almost all houses that are available
- Color pictures of the homes listed as well as (sometimes) virtual tours
- Textual descriptions including lot and house sizes, number of bedrooms and baths
- Location of the property, often including a map showing how to get there
- E-mail addresses and phone numbers so that you can communicate with the sellers directly

From the above it should be obvious that you can very quickly scan dozens if not hundreds of listing from the comfort of your computer room. This tends to be far more efficient than trying to look at a listing book in an agent's office. It's certainly more efficient than touring streets hunting for FSBO signs.

On the other hand, once you find a listing you are interested in, it again becomes a physical game. The disadvantages of the Internet include the following:

- You cannot actually see the property or neighborhood. You must view it by physically going to it. This is critically important.

- As of this writing, you cannot easily make binding offers over the Web.

- You should physically go with any professional conducting an inspection of the property to learn firsthand of any problems or defects.

Thus, the Internet is basically a happy hunting ground. It allows you to easily locate properties that you might want to invest in.

Identifying the Bargains among the Properties Listed on the Web

That, of course, is the rub. The listings on the Internet can provide loads of information about any given property. But they can't tell you if it's a good buy. To tell if it's a good buy, you must do the same sort of field work that you would do for a paper MLS listing. You have to go to the property and check it out. Talk to the owner or agent. You'll quickly discover what the real truth is about the property.

Of course, once you find a property you like, the Internet can help you confirm your first judgment. You can find Web sites to help you locate comparables sold in the neighborhood, information on schools and crime, title reports, and home inspectors. It's simply a matter of locating a Web site that caters to what you need. Two that I have found helpful in terms of providing investor services are dataquick.com and monsterdata.com.

Work Foreclosures and REOs

Everyone has heard about *foreclosures*, through which an owner loses his or her property to the lender usually for nonpayment of the mortgage. Most people also have heard that if you can pick up a property in foreclosure (as Leslie and David did in the first chapter), you stand to make a good profit. What few people have heard of, however, are REOs. These are properties that have gone through the foreclosure process, are now owned by the bank, and are for sale from the bank.

In this section we'll look at both foreclosures and REOs to see where there's opportunity for investors.

Foreclosures

The Foreclosure Process

Step 1. The seller can't or won't make payments for whatever reason, and the lender puts the mortgage in default.

Step 2. After a legally determined period of time, the lender "sells" the property to the highest bidder "on the courthouse steps."

Step 3. Typically the lender is the highest bidder. It takes control of the property and then attempts to resell it as a real-estate-owned property (REO).

We're going to start with *foreclosures,* described in step 1.

The seller can't or won't make the mortgage payments. He or she is motivated to sell the property hoping to recoup any equity and save a credit rating. This seller is going to at least listen to any offer that you make.

In a strong market, one would think that there simply aren't any sellers in foreclosure. That's simply not the case. The foreclosure rate in good times may be half of what it is in bad times. But in any time there are still plenty of foreclosures. Sellers are always losing property. Some of the more common reasons include the following:

- The seller has overborrowed and can't make the payments.
- There is an illness, death, or divorce in the family, and no one takes charge of maintaining the property, allowing it to fall through the cracks into foreclosure.
- The seller moved and listed the house. But the agent was terrible, and no buyers were found, and now the seller, at a distance, just won't or can't deal with the house anymore.
- The seller simply doesn't care about the property (rare, but it does happen).

Finding Foreclosures   There are many sources of foreclosure listings. Sometimes property listed with an agent will be in foreclosure.

If you find one of these, you know you're dealing with a motivated seller!

Sometimes an FSBO will be in foreclosure. Again, the seller is motivated, but often he or she doesn't have enough equity to pay a listing commission. In that case, it's probably not going to be worth your time. You need to carefully evaluate FSBO foreclosures to determine what the seller's true equity is.

In addition, too often FSBO foreclosure sellers are going this route because they are too stubborn to face facts. They simply won't believe they will soon lose their property, and they continue to insist on an unrealistic price. There's usually very little you can do with an FSBO seller in this frame of mind.

However, occasionally you will find an FSBO who wants to sell and is willing to negotiate realistically. In this case, you may very well be able to pick up a bargain.

Other sources of foreclosures include title insurance companies, who act as trustees in foreclosures. They will often provide a list of foreclosures they are handling.

In addition, there's almost always a local legal newspaper (one that carries legal notices) in which foreclosure notices are published. Pick this up, and you probably will be able to find every foreclosure in town. Be aware, however, that frequently only the *legal* description of the property is given, not the street address. You can get the legal description translated at the county assessor's office, but doing so can be a hassle.

Also, most larger metropolitan areas have a foreclosure bulletin. This is a private publication that lists all foreclosures, and it gives street addresses, names, dates, and so forth. It's everything you need; however, it usually costs a lot, typically several hundred dollars a year to subscribe.

Finally, a number of Web sites deal almost exclusively in foreclosures and REOs. For example, you can try brucebates.com or realtytrac.com. When using any site, however, be sure to check that the foreclosure is indeed in your area.

Acting on a Foreclosure   Once you find someone who is in foreclosure, it is then up to you to contact him or her directly and find out if there is a good deal available for you. Hopefully you already have a name and phone number. Now, just give this person a call. Explain that you're an investor and that you're looking for property in the area. You heard he or she was having some difficulty in making payments and you're wondering if there's a way to make a "win-win" situation out of it—the seller gets to save his or her credit (plus, perhaps, some money depending on the seller's equity) and you get the property.

TRAP

Some people in foreclosure are quite bitter about it. They won't want to talk with you. They may be nasty, even offensive. They usually take their foreclosure personally and may blame everyone but themselves for it. Forget them. They can't be helped and most likely will lose their house and their credit.

What you can offer to the owner is to make up the back payments and penalties and save the owner's credit rating in exchange for the title to the property. In other words, you can offer to take it over. The advantage here is that you get the property for virtually no money down plus whatever equity the owner may have. The disadvantage is that the loan may not be assumable. If that's the case, you may not only have to make up back payments and penalties but also secure a new loan with accompanying points and fees. In short, it may cost you many thousands of dollars to take over this property and bail out this owner. You may find that by the time you add up the costs, it simply isn't worthwhile.

TRAP

The following costs are likely to be incurred in the process of righting a foreclosure:

1. *Back payments.* These could amount to as much as six months of payments or more.

2. *Penalties.* Each month that the payment is late usually incurs a penalty. In addition, there may be additional penalties as time periods in the foreclosure process expire.

3. *New loan costs including points, fees, title insurance, etc.* Typically these costs will add up to about 5 percent of the loan amount. On a $100,000 mortgage, figure about $5,000.

4. *Fixing up the property.* The former owner may not have kept the place in great shape once he or she learned of the foreclosure. You could have to spend several thousands in refurbishing and relandscaping.

It's important that you calculate these costs as accurately as possible before you make any kind of offer to the owner. You may find that it simply isn't worth your time to attempt to right the foreclosure and take over the property.

TRAP

 Some states offer owners a kind of redemption period if they sell their house while in foreclosure. Check in your area. If it exists, it could mean that the seller could come back later—sometimes even years later— and stake a claim on the property! Additionally, you may be required to give the seller a rescission period of 5 days or more during which he or she can take back an agreement to sell. Check with a good agent or attorney in your area for pitfalls such as these.

The Foreclosure Sale   Can I buy at the foreclosure sale? Yes, you can. You can purchase the property when it is sold "on the court-house steps." At the time of the foreclosure sale, the lender always offers the full price of the mortgage (or trust deed). But there is nothing to prevent you or anyone else from offering more.

Your offer, however, usually must be in the form of cash, so you will have to work out financing in advance. And you will often receive no title insurance or other guarantees as to the status of the property. (You might, for example, think you're bidding on a first mortgage only to find that it's a second or third. This could be catastrophic for you.)

Buying at foreclosure sales is a tricky business and is best left to those who are experienced in the field. If you're really interested in it, try to find an attorney who specializes in this and work with him or her. (Also check into my book, *Finding Hidden Real Estate Bargains,* McGraw-Hill, 2002.)

REOs

REO stands for "real estate owned." It refers to property that a lender has taken back through foreclosure.

Lenders hate this kind of property because on their books it shows up as a liability instead of as an asset. Therefore, they are very anxious to get rid of it. However, they are not so anxious that they're willing to take a loss, if there's any way to avert it.

There's a big advantage for a buyer in dealing with a lender rather than a home seller in foreclosure—it's a clean deal with the bank. There's no crying or recriminations. Also, you can get title insurance, and sometimes the bank will even help you with the financing!

In fact, REOs can be wonderful opportunities. The trick is finding out about them. Strangely, most lenders won't admit publicly that they have an REO problem. Many won't admit they even have any REOs. Thus, you can't usually just walk in and ask to buy one.

This secrecy certainly seems to work against the lender's best interests, at least on the surface. One would think that the lender would be out there advertising those properties as heavily as possible. Yet, the lender doesn't. Do you ever recall seeing a lender advertising under its own name for REO buyers? It usually just doesn't happen. (Most of the public isn't even familiar with the term "REO.") The reasoning of the lenders is threefold, as follows.

First, a lender doesn't want to alert federal watchdogs that it has an REO problem. Keeping up a good face can mean the difference between considered to be in business or insolvent.

Second, depositors are wary about where they place their money. Yes, we know every account is guaranteed to $100,000. But how many of us want to put that guarantee to the test? We might bolt if we thought the lender were shaky. In addition, there are holders of amounts larger than $100,000 who frequently move funds lender to lender in an effort to tie up the highest interest rates. These large depositors are not insured, and they will pull their funds at the slightest whiff of trouble from a lending institution. Hence, lenders are very careful not to admit they have many REOs, if for no other reason than to protect their own image.

Third, there is the matter of the real estate market. If it were to be widely known that a lender had an overhang of homes ready to dump on the market in a particular area, that information could adversely affect prices. This would backfire for the lender since it would lower the prices for the properties it was trying to sell.

Finding REOs The truth is that while lenders keep quiet about REOs as far as the general public is concerned, they are often open about them to legitimate investors. After all, they do want to sell them in order to get the money reinvested in a mortgage. You, as an investor, therefore, have to convince the lender that you're a legitimate buyer. What you have to do to find REOs is both tedious and simple. It's tedious because you have to do it over and over again for each lender. It's simple because the process is quite easy.

Basically you need to let a lender know that you are a sophisticated investor. You need to impress on the lender that you understand what an REO is and that you'd like to bid on one. Once the lender understands that you're special and not part of the public only interested in deposits, the lender will open up, at least in a limited way.

Therefore, you need to call the lender and ask for the officer who deals with REOs. Then you need to make a case that you're an investor who has the means and desire to purchase.

Sometimes you'll be told that this particular lender handles all REOs through a specific real estate broker. You'll have to contact the broker. Other times you'll learn that the lender handles the REOs itself and there's a list of such properties. You'll want to get the list.

Checking Out the REO It's common to find REOs in distressed condition. After all, if you were the borrower and were losing the house, your equity, and your credit rating, would you be anxious to keep watering the lawn or to clean up when you left?

Borrowers who lose their property through foreclosure tend to stop taking care of the property, and some actually go out of their way to mess up the property. Their reaction, naturally enough, is anger, and since they really can't take it out on anyone personally, they typically take it out on the property.

When you get to inspect the REO, it may still be in the terrible shape in which the lender got it back. Or it may be fixed up. Lenders are not fools. They know that a distressed property will get them a distressed price. On the other hand, if they fix it up even just cos-metically, they stand to get a far better price. However, if you arrive on the spot just as the REO is acquired and offer to take it "as is," the lender may agree. After all, time spent fixing up the property is, once again, lost interest to the lender.

When you find an REO in distressed condition, don't turn your head away in disgust. You may not be looking at a disaster but rather at an opportunity

Buying an REO   Buying an REO is like buying any other property. You make an offer to the lender. If it likes your offer, you've got a deal. If it doesn't, you can try to negotiate.

Most lenders prefer all cash. That way they get rid of the proper-ty once and for all. This simply means that you have to go to a dif-ferent lender to get financing. However, don't expect great financing on REOs. Typically you'll be looking at 10 percent down or more, plus closing costs.

On the other hand, some lenders recognize the fact that they will get less from a cash offer, so they agree to handle the financing themselves, for a higher sales price. Sometimes they'll even throw in a cash credit toward having the property fixed up!

If the lender handles the financing, you'll often get the benefits of a lower down payment and easier terms plus, perhaps, some fix-up money. On the other hand, you'll probably pay more than you would if you were buying strictly for cash.

Problems to Expect When Buying an REO   Expect distressed prop-erties. They are more the rule than the exception. That means you have to be very careful to check out an REO and determine your cost to fix it up. Some properties are simply hopeless. A lender may give you a terrific deal on these, but beware of what you're getting.

As Is. Most REOs are sold "as is," even if the lender has refurbished it. The lender-seller makes no warranty to you of any kind. This means that later on, after the sale, if you discover a problem that costs $10,000 to fix, it's your headache, not the lender's. (That's why the price is cheaper!)

Without Disclosures. While most states now require sellers to pro-vide disclosure statements, this regulation may not apply to a lender who is federally chartered. This type of lender may refuse to give you any kind of disclosure statement except one that the federal government requires (on lead, for example). After all, the lender itself may have next to no knowledge about the condition of the property.

Or, if you do get a disclosure from a lender, it may disclose virtually nothing, the lender claiming it knows nothing about the property. Once again, you're on your own.

No Repairs. Certainly, you'll want to get a home inspection. In fact, you'll want the most thorough inspector you can find. However, don't expect the lender to do anything toward correcting problems the inspector finds. Typically, beyond basic refurbishing, most lenders will make no repairs of any kind, even if the inspector finds safety issues. (In that case, the lender may insist you sign a statement that you accept the property at your own risk!)

REOs offer profits, sometimes big profits. But they are certainly not without risks. I wouldn't recommend them for the very first time investor. But once you've gotten your feet wet buying and selling a few properties, you may find that REOs are worth the challenge.

Check Out Government Repos

The government owns a tremendous amount of real estate, almost all of it in the form of houses. However, it doesn't want this property, so it's always trying to sell it. You can sometimes take advantage of these sales to get into a property at a bargain price.

Below is a list of the more popular government repo programs and how to acquire the properties.

HUD Repos

The Housing and Urban Development (HUD) Department takes back homes mainly through its FHA program. The FHA insures lenders who make loans. When a borrower defaults, the FHA makes good the loan to the lender, and it takes the property back. At any given time, it may have tens of thousands of repoed homes for sale across the country. You can check to see if there are any HUD homes in your area on the Internet at hud.gov.

Since the homes come back mainly through the FHA program and since that program has a maximum loan amount as of this writing of around $240,000, you're not likely to find many upscale properties here. Most are going to be in the moderate to low price range.

Additionally, the homes may not be in the best condition. HUD usually does not fix up the properties. That means that they may be in anywhere from average to really bad shape. Don't be surprised at the terrible condition in which you may find a HUD home. Remember that the former owner lost the property to foreclosure, and there was little incentive to keep it up. Additionally, since that time there may have been vandalism.

Making an Offer As noted, you must make your offer through an agent who represents HUD in your local area. Once you locate a home that you're interested in, contact the referred agent and go see the property. The agent can arrange to have you walk through. You'll also make your offer directly through the agent.

Pricing HUD tries to sell its homes at fair market price. However, sometimes this price is difficult to determine because of the run-down condition of the properties. Occasionally, particularly if you are sharp at knowing property values, you can find some real bargains here! (Check into the next chapter for tips on how to scout out run-down properties.)

Financing HUD doesn't make loans directly, but it does work with lenders in a variety of programs. You may be able to get in with virtually nothing down, as long as you intend to occupy the home. If you're buying as an investment, HUD will usually want at least 10 percent down. In other words, your financing needs are going to be similar to those for any investment property. (Look into the next section for tips on getting investment loans.) HUD often looks with extra favor on buyers who submit offers that are a cash-out to HUD. In other words, you get your own outside financing.

Owner-Occupants

As do many government programs, HUD aims to sell its homes to those who will occupy them. Read NOT to investors. Thus in the initial "offer period," HUD looks at offers from those who intend to occupy the homes for sale in the HUD program. If you're looking for both a house to live in *and* invest in, this can be the perfect choice for you.

Investors   However, if no owner-occupants submit offers during the initial offer period, or if the home does not sell in that time frame, then investors can make offers that will be considered.

Does this mean that you as an investor have a chance at buying only the leftovers? Not really. Remember, most of these homes are not in great shape, and most owner-occupants are not eager to buy into them. Further, remember that HUD makes an effort to offer the homes at market price. For casual home owner-occupant buyers who don't really know the market, it may not seem like there are any bargains here.

As a result, very often these homes are sold to investors.

Fix-Up Allowance   If the home is in bad shape, HUD may offer a fix-up allowance. This can be in the form of either an additional price reduction or a special fix-up loan. However, in order to get this, you must be sure it's part of your purchase offer. Once you've made your offer and it's accepted by HUD, it's too late to request a fix-up allowance.

Bonuses   HUD may also offer special incentives if it's particularly interested in moving a property. For owner-occupants, these incentives can include a moving allowance. For investors, these incentives can include a bonus (price reduction) for closing the sale fast. If you have all your financing ducks in a row and can close within a week or two, you might realize a significant financial gain.

Professional Inspection   To avoid buying a "pig in a poke," you'll want to have a professional inspection of the home. However, unlike conventional purchases in which the professional inspection is normally conducted *after* you've signed a purchase agreement with the seller, when you work with HUD, you need to make your inspection *beforehand.* HUD doesn't like to tie up homes on contingencies that involve inspections.

As noted, at any given time, there are thousands of HUD homes for sale in virtually every state. If you're interested in working the repo market, you owe it to yourself to check out the HUD program.

VA Repos

The Veteran's Administration (VA) has an extensive program of loan guarantees. Unlike HUD, which *insures* loans to lenders, the VA *guarantees* the performance of a loan to a lender. (Actually, it guarantees only a small percentage of the top of the loan.) If the borrower defaults, the VA pays off its guaranteed portion. However, rather than simply pay out cash, the VA, because it has determined that it is more profitable to do so, actually buys the property from the lender who forecloses and then resells it.

Initially only those veterans who qualify (were on active duty during specific time periods) can get VA loans in order to buy a home. After the VA has foreclosed, however, it opens the sale to anyone, veteran or nonveteran, investor or owner-occupant.

As of this writing, the VA has over 21,000 homes for sale nationwide in its inventory, and it is averaging over nine months to sell them.

Making an Offer To purchase a VA home, as you would with the HUD program, you must go through a local real estate agent who represents the VA's property management program. Typically these agents will advertise in local newspapers.

You may also find most, but not all, of the properties listed on the VA's property management Web site. Unlike HUD, the VA does not maintain an Internet presence with a list of all properties. It is up to the local property management office to determine whether to link to the VA site and whether to list its homes on the Web. Check out homeloans.va.gov.

To make an actual offer, you must go through an agent and use the proper forms. These include the following:

- Offer to purchase/contract of sale (VA form 26-6705)
- Credit statement (VA form 26-6705B)

Financing The VA will handle some financing. However, it prefers to do this for owner-occupants. And it gives priority to buyers who come in with their own financing (cash to the VA). You will usually, though not always, do better if you handle your own financing outside the VA.

Condition of the Property As is true for homes in the HUD programs, many VA properties are in the same condition they were in when they were turned over after foreclosure. In the past, however, the VA has had an extensive program of refurbishing properties in order to get a higher market value. If you buy a refurbished home, don't expect to get any kind of bargain on the price. How the homes are handled is determined largely by the regional VA property management office.

Inspection Again, you'll want to have a professional inspection so that you'll know what you're getting. However, as with HUD, you'll need to conduct the inspection during the offering period, not after your offer has been accepted. The agent who is handling the house can arrange for you and your inspector to see the property. Be sure you use a sharp pencil when you calculate how much the property is really worth.

The VA program has been in existence for over 50 years. I've been involved with it at different times and in different ways, and I have seen many owners obtain solid investment property through it.

Fannie Mae Properties

Fannie Mae, along with Freddie Mac discussed next, are the main secondary lenders in the country. They underwrite most of the conventional (non-government-insured or guaranteed) mortgages that are made. What this means is that when you get a mortgage from, say, XYZ lender, the lender then in effect sells your mortgage to Fannie Mae or Freddie Mac from which it receives enough money to go out and make additional mortgages.

If, however, you fail to make your mortgage payments and fall into foreclosure, it's Fannie Mae or Freddie Mac (through whatever lender happens to be servicing the mortgage at the time) that takes the property back. Those agencies then have to get rid of it, similar to the way in which HUD or the VA must dispose of their properties. This, again, can present an opportunity for investors.

Property Types Fannie Mae underwrites all types of single-family homes, which include detached properties, condos, and town houses. Most of their inventory consists of fairly new homes that are often in modest to even upscale neighborhoods. My own observation is that the Fannie Mae properties tend to be a little classier than either the HUD or VA homes.

Property Listings   As with HUD and the VA, Fannie Mae requires you to go through a local real estate agent. However, the agents are required to list all the homes on the local MLS, so there's no difficulty in gaining access. Any agent on the local board can show you the home, as well as make the offer for you. Your offer will then go to the listing agent who will in turn present it to Fannie Mae.

You can also find a list of Fannie Mae homes at its Web site: fanniemae.com/homes

Making an Offer   The transaction is handled just as if you were dealing with any other conventional seller. Fannie Mae can accept, reject, or counter your offer. Indeed, you may go through several rounds of countering before the deal is finally done.

Unlike negotiations with either HUD or the VA, you can add contingencies and other conditions with your offer to Fannie Mae. You may ask to have a professional home inspection *after* the offer is accepted. You can also negotiate over terms, down payment, and financing. Fannie Mae will not, however, accept a contingency that requires the prior sale of a seller's current home.

You may use your own title insurance and escrow company. However, to have your offer accepted, you must usually be preapproved by a lender. That means that you've had your credit checked and your income and cash-on-deposit verified.

Condition of the Property   These are repos, which means they may (or may not) be in poor condition. Sometimes Fannie Mae will fix up these properties in order to get a higher price. Other times Fannie Mae will leave them in the condition in which they received them. In any event, all the homes are sold in "as-is" condition, meaning that the buyers must take the homes with whatever problems they have at the time of sale.

Financing   Fannie Mae does offer its own REO financing. However, it's typically not any better than you would get elsewhere. Further, you may have a better chance of getting your offer accepted if you come in with cash to Fannie Mae (that is, if you secure outside financing).

As with other government repo programs, to get a bargain, you must be on top of the market. You must be able to recognize true value where others miss it. Making a sharp offer can often net you an excellent deal.

Freddie Mac Properties

Like Fannie Mae, Freddie Mac offers single-family detached homes, condominium units, and town houses. However, Freddie Mac often cleans and fixes up its homes before offering them for sale. If you want to submit an offer on a home for which you propose doing the fix-up work yourself, chances are the Freddie Mac will still at the least clean up the property to some extent before you buy it.

Through its HomeSteps program, Freddie Mac will offer homes to owner-occupants at competitive interest rates with 5 percent low down payments and no mortgage insurance. It will also offset some of the title and escrow costs. These homes, however, are almost all competitively priced at market.

Freddie Mac homes are offered through a select group of lenders. To find out more about them, check out the Web site homesteps.com.

Other Government Repo Programs

There are many other government repo programs including some from the IRS as well as local government authorities. The following list may help you in checking them out.

TIP

You're best off checking these out at their Web sites. If you call, you could spend hours trying to reach the right person with the correct information. The Web sites, on the other hand, are generally organized to give you the information you need right away.

- *Customs.* treas.gov/auction.customs.html
- *Department of Veteran Affairs.* homeloans.va.gov/homes

- *Federal Deposit Insurance Corporation.* fdic.gov/buying/owner/index
- *U.S. General Services Administration.* propertydisposal.gsa.gov/property/propforsale.html
- *Internal Revenue Service.* treas.gov/auctions/irs/real.html
- *Small Business Administration.* appl.sba.gov/pfsales/dsp_search.html
- *U.S. Marshals Service.* usdoj.gov/marshals/assets/nsl.html
- *U.S. Army Corps of Engineers.* sas.usace.armyu.mil/hapinv/haphomes.html

4

Evaluating Cash Flow

This chapter grew out of an e-mail that I received at my Web site (robertirwin.com) from a reader complaining that he was having trouble getting a property's rental income to cover the mortgage and other expenses. "How do I know *in advance* whether a property I'm interested in buying is an alligator or a cash cow? And how do I reduce negative cash flow in a rental property I already own?" he asked.

An *alligator* is a property for which your expenses are so high that you can't cover them with the rental income, and your monthly losses (*negative cash flow*) eat you alive, hence the name. A *cash cow* is a property for which your rental income exceeds your expenses, and each month, it gives you "milk" in the form of money in your pocket (*positive cash flow*).

In this chapter, we'll look at some solutions to the age-old problem of evaluating investment property in terms of its cash flow.

How Do I Calculate Income versus Expenses?

If you are planning to invest in real estate, it's important that you understand exactly what your expenses are likely to be. If you already own investment property, you need to know at all times where you stand financially vis-à-vis your investment. (Income is much easier to estimate or determine—unless you have a vending machine or two, it's simply the total of your rents for the property.) A useful tool in both situations is the *rental property income and expense sheet*.

At the end of every month, for a rental property you already own, you can draw up an income and expense report to help gauge the status of your cash flow. These figures will give you a very exacting look at how well you did that month. If you haven't been sufficiently careful, your ledger could look like the one that follows:

Monthly Rental Property Income and Expense Sheet

Income (from rent) $1,500		$1,500
Expenses		
Mortgage payment	$1,500	
Taxes	600	
Insurance	50	
Maintenance	50	
Repairs	50	
	2,250	–$2,250
Monthly cash loss		–750
Depreciation	500	
Monthly expense *after* depreciation	2,750	–2,750
Monthly loss *with* depreciation		–1,250

This property is losing $750 *cash* a month not including depreciation. That's a loss of $9,000 a year! Nobody in his or her right mind would want such an alligator. Indeed, this is the type of negative cash flow that eats you alive!

But, some readers may be wondering, what about tax shelters? Doesn't rental real estate provide some tax benefits for owners?

How Do I Calculate the Tax Benefit?

Note: determining the tax benefits of owning a particular piece of real estate can be a task requiring a high level of expertise. The following discussion is intended strictly as an overview and might not apply in your situation. Before making any move that would involve tax consequences, see a good accountant or tax attorney.

Like most people, you have probably heard that real estate ownership can provide a tax shelter. Don't the tax advantages offset the monthly cash loss?

No, not entirely, at least not in most cases. It's true that you may get some tax advantages out of owning rental realty. Virtually all the expenses in our example (with the exception of the principal portion of the mortgage payment, that which repays the loan) can be used to offset your rental income for the purpose of determining your profit. When you add to that an amount for depreciation (shown above),your monthly expenses could exceed your monthly income (in our example, that is the case—by well over a thousand dollars). That amount— a loss—*might* be deductible from your other taxed income.

TIP

It's important to understand that, when calculating your profit or loss, rental expenses must first be offset by rental income. You can't simply take all your rental property expenses as a deduction from your total taxable income from all sources combined. For your investment rental property, you first subtract your property expenses from your property income, and if that reveals a loss, that loss *may* be deductible against your total taxable income.

For the above property, each month we have a $1,250 loss after depreciation. How much of a tax advantage is that?

The answer depends on several factors including your total income and your marginal tax bracket. For now, let's just say that if your total annual income is $150,000 or higher, you will *not* be able to take any immediate tax deductions for your rental property. In other words, for practical purposes there are no immediate tax deduction advantages from investment property for those who are well off enough to make over $150,000 a year. (It all has to do with the "active-passive" rules of the tax code. Remember that this is a very superficial look at real estate taxation in which we are glossing over many of the details. For a more thorough examination, check into Chapter 12.)

If your annual income, on the other hand, is under $150,000, then you may be able to deduct at least a part of your loss from that year's income. In other words, the property will provide a tax benefit.

How big is the tax benefit likely to be? That's determined by your marginal tax bracket. The higher your bracket, the greater the benefit.

Let's say that you're in the 28 percent tax bracket. (Check with your accountant to see what your marginal bracket is—you might be surprised to find it's lower than you think!) You could get 28 percent of the $1,250 monthly loss, or $350 a month, in our above example. Doing so would yield the following:

Estimated Tax Savings

Monthly loss	$1,250
Tax bracket	× 28 percent
	350
Annualized	× 12 percent
	$4,200

On this property, assuming a 28 percent tax bracket, the actual tax savings (the amount you'll not have to pay in taxes) would be slightly over $4,000.

TRAP

Another mistake that first-time investors sometimes make is to think that the rental property loss can simply be deducted from the taxes owed to the federal government. It cannot. A rental property loss is deducted from the rental property owner's gross personal income. The loss is not subtracted from the total taxes the property owner is paying for the year. That means the loss offsets the other income you make, not the taxes you pay. To calculate it, you must first multiply it times your tax bracket, as indicated above.

Being able to deduct $4,200 from your annual taxable income does help a lot to offset the $9,000 annual loss. Suddenly that loss is down to about $5,000. But even that is high, and most people would still consider a property with that much loss to be an alligator.

So the question becomes how to get that loss reduced so that the owner at least breaks even? In other words, how can a rental property owner deal with negative cash flow?

Can I Increase the Rents?

If your rents aren't enough to cover expenses, why not just increase rents? The answer to that question depends on the amount of leeway there is between the rent you are charging and the rent most other rental property owners in your area are charging. In the real world in the open market for rental units, you are in competition with every other landlord-investor. Increase your rents beyond the prevailing market rates and you'll have nothing but vacancies.

That's the case once you already own the property. However, there are some things you can do to avoid a negative cash flow problem before you buy. For example, buy a less expensive property for which your mortgage, taxes, and insurance—that is, your expenses—will be lower than your rental income.

TIP

Your constant goal should be to buy a rental property close to break-even.

I'm sure many readers will be quick to point out that if you pay less for a property, you will get less rental income from it. So even though your expenses will go down (because of a lower purchase price), so too will your rental income.

Yes—and no. Renting is different from buying and selling. In the sale and purchase market, the price is usually well defined for each property, being controlled to a certain extent by lending practices in the area. For example, you can get a CMA (comparative market analysis) that will pinpoint the value of the home. With rentals it's less clear. For example, a three-bedroom two-bath home may rent fairly consistently for around $1,000 in your area. However, homes with three bedrooms and two baths may sell anywhere from $120,000 to $160,000 in the same area. In other words, if you buy a three and two at the lower end of the price range, you'll very likely still be able to rent it for roughly the same amount as if you had bought the property at the upper end of the price range. Yet your monthly expenses will be far less in the lower-priced property. So one way to lower your monthly expenses is to "buy right" in the first place.

Can I Cut Expenses?

Assuming you've done all you can to increase your rental income, is there anything else you can do to get closer to break even on a property you already own? Can you cut your expenses? That, of course, is the big question. Here are the answers using the property described above as an example:

Fixed Expenses

Taxes   There's very little you can do to cut your property taxes. It might be possible to have the property reassessed, but unless market values overall have dropped, a revaluation is just as likely to result in a higher assessment as in a lower one. This is most likely a fixed expense that you have to pay.

Insurance   As with taxes, insurance tends to be a fixed expense. You could shop around for a cheaper policy. But remember, in addition to fire insurance, as a landlord you also need high liability insurance in case a tenant gets hurt on the property and sues you. Again, there's probably little you can do here.

Maintenance   This item covers routine expenses such as paying the water bill and lawn, pool, and garden care services. Actually, $50 is very low. It's unlikely you'll be able to cut this figure significantly.

Repairs   This expense is actually a reserve. You put away 50 bucks a month so that when a $500 water heater goes out, you have the cash to pay for it. If the house is much older, $50 a month is probably not enough. You might have to put away several hundred dollars a month to be ready to repair a roof or heating system. If the house is nearly new and in good shape, you might be able to reduce this reserve.

TIP

A wise investor will also keep a reserve for clean-up, rent loss, and rent up. Most landlords assume their property, on average, will be vacant between two and four weeks a year as tenants come and go. Each time a tenant moves out, there's a *clean-up* expense. Then, until a new tenant moves in, there's a *rent-loss* expense. And finally, to find a new tenant, there's advertising, credit reports, and other *rent-up* expenses.

Variable Expense: The Mortgage

We are left with only one expense that we can control in some way: the mortgage payment.

We can reduce the mortgage payment in a variety of ways. We've already discussed buying a less expensive home and putting in more of your own cash. Here are some other techniques.

Another way to reduce the mortgage payment is to get a lower interest rate. There are a variety of ways to do this. You can plan ahead so that if interest rates are high when you make your purchase, you can go for an adjustable rate loan. This type of loan typically begins with a "teaser" rate that is below market, often as much as 1 to 3 percent or more lower. The savings can be huge. Just keep in mind, however, that these teaser rates disappear rather quickly. Often within a year or two your interest rate on the adjustable loan will rise to market or even above. That's the time to refinance, if possible, to a lower-rate mortgage (or to resell).

On the other hand, if interest rates happen to be low when you buy, get a fixed-rate 30-year loan. This will lock your mortgage into the low rate so that when interest rates rise, you won't find your monthly expenses going up.

TIP

With investment property, almost always go for the longest-term mortgage you can get—typically 30 years. The reason is your goal of low monthly payments to reduce your overall monthly expenses. Shorter-term loans are sometimes written with a slightly lower interest rate and a greater return on equity, but the payments are always higher. Go for the long-term mortgage.

Yet another way to reduce the mortgage amount—and thereby reduce your monthly mortgage expense—is to get rid of the PMI. In our examples in which we obtained a low to zero down mortgage by being an owner-occupant, we glossed over the fact that these mortgages all come with private mortgage insurance (PMI). This insures the lender (not you, the borrower) against loss in case you fail to make your payments. You, however, pay the cost in terms of a higher interest rate, typically ⅜ to ¾ percent more. This can add $100 or more to your monthly mortgage payment.

There are two ways to get rid of the PMI. The first is to prove to the lender that your home has appreciated in value to the point where the mortgage is less than 80 percent of the value. At that point, the lender should simply take off the PMI, which will lower your payments. However, it takes time for the value of your house to appreciate sufficiently, often many years.

Another method is to refinance. Here you get two smaller loans instead of the original large one. You get a first mortgage for 80 percent of the value (remember, no PMI required here) and a second mortgage for as high as possible, anywhere from 10 to the full remaining 20 percent of the property's current value. Hopefully the combined interest rate of the two mortgages will be less than the rate for the large single mortgage with PMI. Any good mortgage broker can run the numbers for you. (Also, check into Chapter 13 where we'll go into financing in greater detail.)

Obviously, it's not going to be easy to cut the mortgage expense. But there is another way to do it: Put more cash down.

Can I Cut the Mortgage Expense by Putting More Money Down?

It's important to understand the relationship between how much you put into the property and your monthly expenses. The less you put of your own money into a property, the greater your leverage and, ultimately, your profits. However, your monthly expenses will be greater too because you'll have a bigger mortgage.

On the other hand, the more you put of your money into a property, the lower will be your mortgage payments—and the less difficulty you'll have in covering them with rental income. Put more down and you'll have lower mortgage payments, which, of course, are much easier to meet.

TRAP

One of the biggest mistakes that first-time real estate investors make is to underestimate their mortgage expense and overestimate their rental income.

But doesn't this fly in the face of the advice that says use other people's money (OPM)? The more of your own money you put in, the less of OPM you're using. Won't that reduce your profits?

Yes, and no. Your profits will also be reduced if each month you need to put money into a property to keep it out of foreclosure (in other words, if you need to make huge payments not covered by rental income). Put less money down, and you might get nickel and dimed to death.

It's important to remember that buying and renting real estate is a balancing act. The closer you get to breakeven, the better an investment your property is. The ideal rental investment, in fact, will break even or produce a positive cash flow.

Thus, use as much of OPM as you can. But balance that with your own money (after buying right and getting the lowest mortgage payment possible through wise financing).

Is there any other time when putting in more cash makes sense? As we've said, if you can to find a property that offers high rent with low expenses and you finance the property wisely, you can get by putting in little to no cash of your own. On the other hand, if you buy a property with a lower rental income and higher payments, you'll want to put your money into it to reduce the mortgage amount to where the monthly payments are balanced by the rental income.

Sometimes, however, your goal is not simply to rent the property out but to turn it over for a big profit. When properties are appreciating rapidly, you may need a time frame of only a year or two, sometimes much less. During that time you hope to resell for a big profit, to make a killing on a market upswing. So you may overlook the goal of buying close to breakeven and instead buy a property for which the rental income doesn't come close to meeting the expenses. In this sort of situation, putting in a lot of cash to keep the mortgage payments low can make sense.

Think of it this way: *If you have the cash*, what else would you do with it? Your choices are limited: stocks, bonds, and interest-bearing deposits. Chances are you'll make far more on it by putting it into a piece of real estate that has the potential to generate a quick profit. (Besides, with lots of cash and a quick buy, you can sometimes persuade the seller to significantly reduce the price.)

I've known investors who would put as much as 50 percent, sometimes 100 percent, down on a short time frame with the intent of reselling. Ultimately, your decisions will line up with your investment goals.

As we've seen, you can determine a property's cash flow by careful analysis, before you buy. If you need to lower a negative cash flow for a property you already own, you can do so in the ways that we've suggested. However, always keep in mind that some properties simply will never break even or produce a positive cash flow no matter what you do, short of paying the entire price for them in cash.

5

Working with Agents

Starting out in real estate investing is just like starting out in anything else: Because it's all new, at first you're going to be at a disadvantage. You won't know the area, the way deals are constructed, what to expect in the paperwork, and so on. That's why I suggest that first-time investors do *not* go it alone.

Reading a book like this will certainly help get you up to speed on how things are done. However, for advice on your specific location and on specific deals that you're considering, you need a professional. In short, you need a real estate agent.

This is not to say that you'll always need an agent. In the first chapter we saw how Leslie and David benefited from the agent's (Leo's) advice. However, as they became more conversant with transactions, they needed his aid less and less, until they were finding and managing transactions entirely on their own.

Similarly, you would be wise to find a trusted real estate agent in your area who can lead you by the hand, so to speak, through your first few transactions. How to find that agent, and how much to pay him or her, is what we'll discuss in this chapter.

How Do I Find an Agent I Can Trust?

Everyone who buys or sells property asks himself or herself this question. However, the question takes on a slightly different meaning for an investor. You not only want an agent who is trustworthy in the sense of looking out for your interests, someone who is straightforward and honest, but you also want an agent who has experience you can trust. This means someone who has been in the business a long time, who has seen it all, who can advise you not just on buying a home but on investing as well. Where do you find this person?

Actually, agents who fit that description do exist and in almost every nook and cranny in the country. However, you may need to separate the wheat from the chaff. While the majority of agents come into the business for a few years to try their hand, only a relative few stick it out for decades and make a career of selling real estate. Nevertheless, every town does have some of these career real estate people.

Traditionally, an agent with so much experience would be found in a one-person office. You could simply ask other agents which of the local agents have been around the longest, or you could call the local real estate board and see if they will tell you which brokerage has the greatest longevity.

However, in today's world, most successful real estate people have gone under the umbrella of a national company such as Coldwell-Banker, Century 21, ReMAX, or Prudential. This is particularly the case in larger metropolitan areas. In these markets, it is harder, but not impossible, to identify the type of agent you're looking for.

TIP

In real estate investing, the most important factor in success is the agent, not the office. It's the person who you're working directly with who will find properties for you, will negotiate your deals, and will look out for you.

How Do I Avoid the Wrong Agent?

First, a word about the type of agent you want to avoid. Many highly successful agents today have a very high profile in the community. They sell a lot of properties, often very high priced ones. And they make no bones about telling everyone of their success. You can see their ads popping up on shopping carts in grocery stores, before the movies start in theaters, and in local magazines and newspapers. Typically they say something like "Number 1 Agent in the Community!" or "Sold Over

One Million Dollars in Homes Last Year!" or "Top Producers." (Today many agents are working as a team, husband and wife or just partners, so you'll see two faces on the ad.)

All of this means that this agent sells a lot of properties and makes a lot of money. But how much they make shouldn't interest you. This is not to say you're looking for agents who don't sell. Rather, it's that you're looking for an agent who will take the time to work with you to find just the right property. My experience is that too many of these "hot" agents just churn and burn. They hop from prospect to prospect, and if you don't buy within the first showing or two, they'll dump you and move on. After all, they have a certain volume of sales to maintain.

Indeed, one hot agent I know tells his clients as soon as he meets them that he's not only the number 1 agent in his area but he is also capable of finding the right house for them on their second trip looking. (The first trip, he says, is to let him determine just what they want.) If they don't buy, or at least make an offer on that second trip, then they aren't really sincere. Indeed, he tells them that unless they buy then, they are wasting his time—he goes to great lengths to make the potential buyers feel guilty for not purchasing! If people don't, in fact, buy, he dumps them and moves on. There are plenty of buyers, he says. Why waste time on those who won't act immediately?

Needless to say, he sells a lot of properties and makes a lot of money. But I can't help wondering if his clients really get what they want. Further, I wonder how well he would serve an investor who wants all sorts of additional information such as the amount a house could rent for, how good the tenant base is in the area, and so on?

As an investor you don't want this type of agent. You don't want to be the victim of someone who processes real estate buyers in haste, whose eye is riveted to his or her bottom line. Rather, you want someone who is successful enough to have the time to invest in his or her clients, who is willing to take as much time as necessary to help them, and who is determined to get for them just what they want.

What Does the Right Agent Look Like?

Typically the right agent for a beginning investor will be someone who's been in the business long enough to become financially secure—a career agent. Ideally this person should own investment properties on his or her own so that he or she knows what it is to invest and to be a landlord. Further, this person should have enough income from his or her own investments that he or she doesn't need to churn and burn, to turn over prospects quickly in order to maintain a high volume and a high income just from sales.

That means that the right agent will probably have the following profile:

Profile of the Right Agent

1. *Middle aged or older.* Remember, it takes a while to build up a string of properties and accumulate wealth in real estate—while there are some very excellent young agents, it's not usually done overnight.

2. *Active in real estate for at least a decade.* There are many private investors who have made their fortune and then turned to selling as an agent as a pastime. They rarely have the people skills to help you. You want someone who's been in the business as an agent for a while, 5 years being the minimum, 10 being better. Beware of beginning agents, those in business less than 5 years. They will be learning on you.

3. *Successful.* It's possible to be in real estate and never really make it. There are a lot of agents who are at the periphery of the field. Typically these agents have outside incomes, perhaps retirement from another field. They dabble in property and occasionally sell a home. But they don't own much property themselves, and they really don't have a handle on how buying and selling for investment is actually done. The worst thing about these agents is that they may give you advice gleaned from their own experience, sometimes *bad* advice!

4. *Willing to take time with you.* The right agent will quickly realize that you're sincere about investing and will also realize that if he or she plays their cards right, you'll buy multiple properties through him or her over a period of many years. In short, they'll understand that you represent a renewable resource. Hence, they'll be willing to assist you, show you properties over many months, suggest courses of action, and so forth. In other words, they'll be interested in a long-term relationship.

5. *Honest, straightforward, and pleasant.* Notwithstanding all of the above qualities, you'll also want your agent to have those characteristics that every agent should have. You'll want him or her to be on your side, always. You'll want to know you can trust what he or she says. And you'll want him or her to be able to get along with you.

TIP

The ideal agent must be assertive enough to tell you when you're wrong and to deal effectively in negotiations with the other party. Beware of agents who are too aggressive. While you may think that you'll be turning them loose on the other party, you may find they are actually asserting enormous pressure on you to act, quickly, and not necessarily on what you really want.

Where Do I Find the Right Agent?

We've already suggested trying to find the agent who has been around in town the longest. However, if real estate in your area is handled predominantly by franchise or national companies, as it is in most places, then I suggest the following procedure:

Finding a Good Agent

- Locate a large office within the area in which you want to buy. (Remember, one of your first tasks is to identify your "farm" or geographic area where you'll buy.) Be sure to go to that office, not another branch of the same company.

- Go into the office and ask to speak to the broker/manager. Each office is typically organized with a broker and a number of salespeople. The broker is the one who runs the show. If you just go in and ask to speak to an "agent" (a generic term that can mean either broker or salesperson) instead of a "broker," you'll get the next person "up." This is the salesperson who's on duty that day, and he or she is often a beginner. Once you are linked to this person, you'll be stuck with him or her. Other agents don't like stepping on the toes of their associates and "stealing" clients.

- When you get to see the broker, explain exactly what you're looking for—the most experienced agent in the office to help you get started investing for the long term. Explain that you don't want a hot shot. You want someone who has the time to explain the business to you. (That person may turn out to be the very broker you're talking to, but probably not, because brokers who run offices rarely have the time to spend with first-time investors. More likely it will be another broker who has "parked" his license there.)

TIP

Experienced brokers will often "park" their license under another broker who runs an office. This means that while they retain the ability to convert back to a broker's status at will, for the moment they are the equivalent of a salesperson. They do this to avoid the expense of operating their own office, as well as to get the benefits of being in an office with a lot of active agents and advertising. . (Note that in some cases experienced lone brokers may *park* their license in another sense, in that they retain their broker's license and simply rent office space from another broker.)

- When you find an agent who you think is a likely candidate to be just right for you, interview him or her. Ask the following questions:
  - How long have you been active in the business selling real estate (not just investing on your own)? A good answer is 10 years or more.
  - Do you invest on your own? If so, how many properties do you have? A good answer would be 10 or more.
  - How may properties have you sold over the past year? (A good number is at least eight. That's only one every month and a half.)
  - Would you be willing to work with me (or us) over the long haul? (A wise broker will wait to answer this until he or she has had time to interview you to see just how sincere you are!)
- When you've found someone you like, test your choice. Go out with this person to look at property. See what he or she suggests you do. Remember, if it turns out you made a mistake, you can always say goodbye and continue your search.

Should I Work with One Agent Exclusively, or Many?

This is an age-old question in real estate that I am constantly asked. Is it better to work with one agent or with several? The answer is, it depends.

When you're first starting out, I suggest that you find one good agent (as explained above) and stick with him or her like glue. Your loyalty to the agent will be paid off by his or her loyalty to you and advice and help that you really need.

However, once you've become an experienced investor, then you may want to work with several agents. Of course, you won't expect the kind of loyalty or attention that you'd receive by working with one agent exclusively. However, by then you may not need it.

When you're an advanced investor, you may want to work with a group of agents in order to have the best chance at finding a specific type of property. (With commercial, industrial, or apartment properties, sometimes agents will keep listings to themselves.) You'll let them know exactly what you're looking for in terms of property and tell them that you're working with others. However, by then they should have confidence that you will buy through the agent who finds what you want. You'll also let them know that you'll pay a buyer's commission (explained below), if necessary, for their efforts. Making this offer will encourage the agents to continue to look for properties that you can use and to call you when they find them.

TIP

Agents value loyalty above all else. The worst insult you can give an agent is to spend hours, days, weeks, and longer with him or her looking at various properties only to then buy through another agent. If you give an agent loyalty-work exclusively through them—very often the agent will reward you with superior service. However, when it comes to investment property, agents also realize that investors are looking for something special that they may not have. They realize that investors will work with several different agents trying to find the right property. While they won't spend a lot of dedicated time looking just for you, if what you want happens to show up, they'll be happy to tell you about it, show it to you, sell it to you, and claim their commission.

Should I Use a "Buyer's Agent"?

Absolutely, especially since you're an investor.

There's been a lot of talk over the last few years about "buyers' agents" versus "sellers' agents," and a lot of the people doing the talking haven't really made clear what the pros and cons are. Be sure you understand the differences.

An agent must declare whom she or he works for. There are three possibilities: the seller, the buyer, or both (called a *dual agency*).

This has nothing to do with who pays the agent. It is perfectly acceptable for the seller to pay an agent who works for the buyer. In fact, it's done all the time.

The reason that it's important that you use a buyer's agent (when you're purchasing property) is that there are important legal and ethical issues involved. If the agent declares for you, then he or she has a fiduciary responsibility to you. This takes many interesting forms. For example, if your agent happens to learn that the sellers are actually willing to accept $20,000 less than their asking price, your agent is duty bound to give you this information. On the other hand, if you're working with a seller's agent, that agent would be duty bound *not* to tell you, and instead to protect the interests of the seller.

Sometimes agents will declare that they are performing in a *dual role*, that is, that they are working for both parties. To my way of thinking, working for both parties is not acceptable. A dual agent is neither fish nor fowl. He or she can't fully represent you without hurting the seller and vice-versa. Thus, the dual agent often ends up trying to shepherd a deal through the pipeline without anyone really getting hurt. The unfortunate result for you, the buyer, is that you're not likely to get what you want: a bargain!

TIP

In almost all states, an agent must declare in writing whom he or she represents. While this can be done at any time before an offer is made, it most certainly should be done at the time you decide to fill out a purchase agreement. And the declaration should be made in writing. (Be sure you save the document. It could come in handy later on if the agent does something harmful to your cause.)

Some excellent agents are able to handle the dual role. But for my money, I'd go with a buyer's agent any day. Which brings up another point, who pays the buyer's agent?

Do I Have to Pay the Buyer's Agent?

If the seller pays the seller's agent, then it stands to reason that the buyer should pay the buyer's agent. However, as noted earlier, that's not how it usually works.

Typically the seller's agent will list a property for, say, a 6 percent commission. The seller's agent will then list the property with the Multiple Listing Service (MLS) or otherwise agree to "cobroker" the property with other agents. This typically means splitting the commission 50-50. Thus, the agent who finds the buyer gets half the commission. (There's no reason that can't be your buyer's agent.) And the seller's agent ends up with half. Thus the seller actually ends up paying your agent.

Sometimes, however, the seller's agent will refuse to cobroker a property. As noted, this occasionally happens in bigger investments such as apartment buildings or commercial or industrial properties. This means that the seller's agent will want the entire commission, or at least the bigger share of it. In that case you might, indeed, need to pay your buyer's agent a commission, or a portion of it. However, in this circumstance hopefully, you won't mind because the deal will be big enough and generate enough profit to make the commission worth your while.

TRAP

Be wary when a buyer's agent asks you to sign an agency agreement. Be sure it does not lock you into paying a commission if the agent can get it from the other side. (You don't want the agent to collect twice, once from the seller and again from you!) You also don't want to make it too easy to get the commission from you, easier than arguing with the seller's agent for it. Also, be sure you're not liable for a commission or fee if you don't buy and that the agreement has a definite termination date. And check to see whether it allows you to work with other agents, or requires you to work exclusively with one.

Can I Ask the Broker to Take Less?

Usually that's a mistake.

It's important to understand that there is no "set" or "fixed" or "standard" commission in real estate. That was done away with decades ago after a series of legal cases. Today, the commission is what the agent and the client agree that it is. And it can be any amount.

However, that being said, most good agents will demand a minimum commission below which they will not work. They may say, for example, that they are worth a full 3 percent (half of a 6 percent commission) and they don't want to work for less. (They will have to split that 3 percent with their office—average agents split it 50-50, but top agents get as much as 80 or 90 percent of their portion of the commission.)

If you then badger them to cut their rate, you're asking them to work for less than they feel they are worth. Some extremely honest agents will simply refuse. They know their value.

Others may grudgingly acquiesce, but you may have poisoned the relationship between you. They will surely resent what you did, and then you'll always be wondering if they are doing as good a job as they should.

TIP

Many people feel that agents get too much money for what they do. The reason some people feel that way is that much of what a good agent does is not visible. A good buyer's agent will spend countless hours checking out property to show you, only to find that most of what he or she sees is just not right for you. When that agent finally shows you, say, three houses, it could be after having previewed three dozen. There's other work as well. There's the agent's expertise in negotiating with the seller, in preparing the purchase agreement, in managing the deal, and in handling the paperwork. And, of course, there's the agent's overhead in maintaining an office, car, advertising, and so on so that he or she can be there ready to go when you need the agent. Commissions are high. But good agents do earn them.

My advice is to do one of two things if you want to pay less. First, of course, find out how much the agent wants. Then, either agree to the amount, or find another agent who is willing to work for less and tells you so right up front.

Should I Use a Discount Agent?

In the past there were very few agents who would work for less than a 6 percent commission. (Years ago most wanted 5 percent, then it went to 6, and in some areas they are now asking 7 percent!) In fact, to help make ends meet, some offices are also trying to tack on a "transaction fee" of several hundred dollars. This extra money does not go to the agent but instead goes to the office to cover its expenses (not covered because it may be paying a top agent 80 to 90 percent of the commission it takes in). I've never met a buyer or seller who was happy about paying a transaction fee, and I expect these will fade away over time.

Today, however, there are many agents in almost all communities who will work on a discount basis, some with very steep discounts. That means that *selling* agents will work for as little as 1 percent (instead of the 3 percent selling agent's typical commission).

Keep in mind, however, that these may not be agents such as Leo, whom we met in the first chapter—they may not be the sort whom you want and need when you first start investing. The reason is that these discounters may compensate for a lower commission by providing less service.

TRAP

One discount franchise company, assist2sell, told me they offer full service for a discount fee, saying they can afford to do so because they have a high volume. You can check them out at assist2sell.com. Their headquarters is in Reno, Nevada, and at the time of this writing, they claim to have about 150 offices nationwide.

If you're going to use a discount broker, be sure you get in writing exactly the services that the broker will perform. And be sure that the services specified are the services you want and need.

Should I Use a Fee-for-Service Broker?

In some areas of the country, a few brokers have taken to advertising that they will perform various parts of a transaction for a set fee. When you arrange with a mechanic to work on your car, the mechanic may charge $1,000 to replace a transmission, $2,000 to overhaul an engine, and so forth. The mechanics fees are spelled out ahead of time. You make arrangements with a fee-for-service broker in the same way.

A fee-for service agent may be all you need, once you are proficient at buying and selling properties and just need a particular service carried out. For example, you may need an agent to draw up the purchase agreement and conduct some negotiations with the seller. You may be willing to pay $500 for that or $1,000. You hire the agent to do just the work you specify, based on his or her fee schedule. Then you do the rest of the work (the escrow, paperwork, and so on) by yourself.

TIP

A fee-for-service arrangement can be particularly useful when you're buying from an FSBO seller who really doesn't know what he or she is doing. By hiring an agent to handle the contact work, you can calm the FSBO seller (who appreciates a professional third party stepping in) and, sometimes, save the deal.

In many parts of the country, attorneys will handle all of the paperwork in a transaction for what amounts to a nominal fee, typically between $750 and $1,500. This represents the biggest bargain in legal services you're likely to find anywhere, and you would be wise to avail yourself of it, if it's an option in your area.

Use an agent when you're just getting started. Choose him or her wisely. And you'll profit in the long run.

6

Cutting Closing Costs

Few agents stress it and even fewer outside the business understand it, but closing costs are the real bane of investing in real estate.

Consider, if you buy or sell stocks or bonds, the transaction charge, even for a full-service brokerage, is likely to be only a few hundred dollars at most. (The fee can be as little as under $30 with a discount stockbroker.) In contrast, with real estate the closing costs are almost always thousands of dollars. For example, a seller who uses a full-service agent can expect to pay around 8 percent of the price of the home in closing costs. For the same property, the buyer's closing costs can be 2 to 4 percent. That means that the combined closing costs for the buyer and seller amount to 10 percent or higher. On a $200,000 home, that's $20,000—a fair piece of change.

TIP

Interestingly, the costs of buying and selling real estate are not called "transaction costs," which is what they are, but instead are called "closing costs." I suspect that's because the latter term is less emotionally charged. A buyer or seller is less likely to complain about the costs involved in "closing the deal" than about the costs involved in "handling the transaction."

For the person who buys and sells a home every decade or so (statistically, people in the United States change homes about once every 8 or 9 years), the closing costs may seem like a lot of money, but not enough to make them change their habits. (When they buy and sell real estate, 85 percent of sellers still use agents and 90 percent of buyers do.)

On the other hand, for the investor who may buy and sell one or more properties every year, these costs can be quite onerous. If you're paying out 10 percent for the round-trip, it's going to take a big bite out of your profits. Therefore, it's very important for the investor to seek ways to reduce those closing costs. We'll see just how you can do that in this chapter.

Negotiating the Closing Costs

In real estate everything is negotiable, including the closing costs. Normally, buyers pay their share and sellers theirs (as determined by local custom). However, there's nothing to prevent your having the other party pay your closing costs.

Why would the other party be willing to do that? Actually, they wouldn't. If I'm selling my house and the buyers ask me to pay their closing costs, my answer is no, what a ridiculous question, case closed.

On the other hand, if the buyers write into the purchase agreement a clause that says their purchase is contingent on my (the seller) paying the closing costs, then it's a slightly different matter. Now it's the case that if I want the deal, I have to pay their costs. If I don't pay their costs, then I chance losing the deal. The buyers, here, have made the closing costs a *deal point* (a deal maker or breaker).

Of course, if you demand something in one area, you're likely to have to give something up in another area. If you ask the sellers to pay your closing costs, chances are they will want you to pay a higher price. What you gain with one hand, you lose with the other, right? Not necessarily.

Remember, as a buyer-investor it's highly unlikely you'll be going in at full price. Instead, you'll low-ball the sellers hoping to pick up the property at a bargain price. All of which is to say that there's probably going to be a lot of negotiation before the final price is agreed upon.

When that's the case, my suggestion is that you do *not* bring up the matter of your closing costs. Rather, you bargain as ruggedly as you can for the price.

If the sellers ultimately agree to your original low-ball figure, then forget about asking them to paying the closing costs. You're already getting the house at a bargain basement price.

On the other hand, what's more likely is that they'll come down some while you come up some. Eventually, the negotiations will reach a crisis. The sellers simply won't come down any further. If you can live with their final price, then at that point agree to it *provided* they pay for your closing costs.

In other words, stop arguing about price and instead turn to terms. It's positively amazing how often sellers will agree to terms if you give them their price.

For example, you may be buying a $300,000 property, and after negotiations you're down to offering $240,000 while they're insisting on $250,000. Only $10,000 separates you.

If you can live with the $250,000 price (a reduction of roughly 17 percent of the asking price—not bad), then agree to it, providing the sellers pay for your closing costs. Since these could be an additional 3 percent, that's another $7,500 thrown your way. Even better, it's in the form of cash that you would otherwise have to come up with. It's $7,500 that you don't have to take out of your pocket to make the deal.

The sales price remains $250,000. However, you get a credit toward your closing costs of $7,500.

Of course, it works both ways. When you're the seller, you can demand that the buyers pay for your closing costs, or a portion of them. (Because of the commission, sellers' closing costs are usually far higher than buyers'.) But, to make the deal, they may be willing to do it.

TRAP

Caution: Sometimes lenders will not go along with one party's paying the recurring costs of another. (*Recurring costs* are such things as interest, insurance, and so forth. *Nonrecurring costs* are such things as commissions and escrow charges.) Be sure you have an agreeable lender. Also, if the sellers pay some of your points, the question arises as to who gets to deduct or capitalize them for tax purposes. Be sure you also first check with your accountant.

Don't think this is an unusual occurrence. It happens in transactions all the time. However, it will never happen unless you insist upon it. Wise investors make it a regular issue to insist that closing costs be part of the deal.

Financing the Closing Costs

A different way to avoid paying the closing costs from out-of-pocket cash is to finance them. Here, instead of the seller's footing the bill, the lender does. Yes, it can work, but you must be careful to find a lender who is agreeable and doubly careful to be sure the lender is fully aware of what's happening. (You don't want an angry lender to later come back and try to either raise your interest rate or rescind your loan because some vital information was held back from them.)

To see how this works, let's assume that you're getting a 90 percent loan (putting down 10 percent of your own money). The property is priced at $200,000 so at full price, the loan amount would be $180,000 with your coming up with $20,000 down. Further, let's say there's an additional $5,000 in costs. The question is, how do you finance that $5,000?

Once again, we're going to assume that as an investor, you're not going to pay full price. Indeed, let's say that after negotiations, you can see that you and the seller will probably agree on a price of around $180,000. That means that you'll need to put down $18,000 with the lender making a new mortgage of $162,000. However, the closing costs are still $5,000.

At this point, you make this offer to the sellers: Instead of a final purchase price of $180,000, you'll pay the sellers the purchase price of $185,000, or $5,000 more. And they, in turn, will give you a $5,000 credit. Is that agreeable?

Notice the difference between this and the previous deal. In that case, the sellers' credit to you for closing costs was below the final price. Here the price is higher.

This shouldn't make any difference to the sellers since they're getting the same money anyhow. However, it will make a big difference to you. At a sales price of $180,000, your mortgage is $162,000. At a sales price of $185,000, the mortgage is now $166,500, or roughly $5,000 more. What you've effectively done is create $5,000 from the mortgage, which will now go to pay your closing costs—you've financed them.

There's no sleight of hand involved. All that's happened is that you're paying a slightly higher price for the property, and the seller, in exchange, is paying your closing costs. It's the same to the seller—you've just got a loan roughly $5,000 higher. As I said, you've financed the closing costs.

Working with the Lender

A lender may object to the transaction just described. The lender may say that the true sales price was $5,000 lower and, thus, so should be the loan.

To my way of thinking, this makes little sense. The loan is (or should be) based on the value of the property as determined by an appraisal. No lender worth its salt will offer a mortgage without an appraisal. And if the property appraises out at the full price (in this case, $185,000), what's the difference how the negotiations went?

In addition, the loan should be based on the *loan to value* (LTV) not on the LTV *plus* closing costs. Thus, as long as you still put the full down payment into the property, in this case 10 percent, you should be meeting the lender's criteria for making the loan.

Nevertheless, if the purchase agreement reflects a price increase at the very end of negotiations, a lender may object saying that the purpose is to get a higher LTV than is warranted on the property. (In all probability the lender is simply worrying that there's some hanky-panky going on that they're not aware of, and they just don't want to take any chances.)

There is a way to avoid this problem. First, find a lender who doesn't object. Many do not. Then, make sure your written offer only reflects the final purchase price. You can simply tell the seller what your final offer will be and why you want it handled the way you do. If the seller agrees, write it up that way.

Getting a Bigger Loan

As mentioned elsewhere in this book, we're living in an age of amazing creativity in financing. Today, the old rules that stipulated 20 percent down no longer apply. Today, if your credit is good enough and your income is sufficiently high, you can get a loan for the entire purchase price of the property. Indeed, in some cases, you can get a loan for 103 percent of the purchase price, meaning that the lender will roll your closing costs into the mortgage.

To find out about 103 percent financing, contact a good mortgage broker. He or she will be able to run the numbers and a credit check to see if you qualify. Keep in mind, however, that this type of financing is available only for owner-occupied property. In other words, you have to intend to live in the property to qualify for that type of financing. If you're buying for investment (that is, you don't plan on living in the house), forget it. The financing available to you probably will be 10 percent down, as indicated above.

Keep in mind that the cost is often higher for financing that includes the closing costs in the mortgage. That means that chances are you'll end up paying a slightly higher interest rate for the mortgage. However, to get the better financing, it's probably worth it.

TRAP

Beware of lenders who offer 125 percent loans. In other words, the mortgage they will sell you will be 25 percent more than the price you are paying for the property. The problem with this type of mortgage is that they may not be just real estate loans but personal loans as well. In other words, you could be personally obligated for repayment regardless of what happens to the property. With a real estate mortgage, normally the property is the only thing you lose if you can't make the payments, and it's unlikely the lender will come after you personally. With a 125 percent mortgage, you could be taking out not only a real estate loan but a personal loan as well, which means that the lender can take action against you personally if you can't keep up the mortgage payments.

Making the Purchase and Sale without a Broker

The biggest single cost in a transaction is usually the broker's commission. This cost is usually paid by the seller, but if a buyer's broker was used, the buyer may have to pay some of the commission as well. If the round-trip costs for a transaction are roughly 10 percent, very often 60 percent of that amount goes to the agent. Obviously, one way to cut costs would be to sell or buy without the services of an agent.

There is nothing wrong with doing this. No one says you must use an agent to handle a real estate transaction for you. However, as we saw in the first chapter, it's very wise to rely on a good agent's experience when you're first getting started. Only a fool would wander into an uncharted wilderness without a guide. You don't want to be that fool when you first get started investing.

On the other hand, once you've got a series of transactions under your belt, it's a different story. Now you've got the experience. And since, as an investor, you're always in the market looking for properties, you may want to handle the entire transaction yourself.

TRAP

Many investors think about getting a real estate license. This is probably *not* a good idea unless you want to actually become an agent. While there's nothing wrong with enrolling in a course that will teach you about real estate, the license itself can be a disadvantage. The reason is that lenders don't like to make their best loans to real estate agents. They know (or suspect) that agents are often making creative deals, and they worry that what's stated on the purchase agreement, which is their guiding document, may not reflect the true deal. This is particularly the case when there's a commission going to one of the parties of the transaction who also happens to be an agent. In short, agents usually get inferior financing. If you're going to invest, just be an investor. You don't need an agent's license.

Keep in mind, however, that while you may know you're competent to handle a real estate transaction, the other party you're dealing with may not be as confident. I've often seen the case in which the seller is perfectly content to sell his property as an FSBO (for sale by owner) but the buyer insists that an agent handle the transaction. Further, in these situations, the buyer sometimes insists that the seller pay that agent's fee, usually half of a full commission, or 3 percent.

You may rail at the seeming unfairness of such constraints because you know what you're doing in acting on your own as a seller and you don't need an agent. But the buyer may simply say to you, No agent, no deal. So in this situation you get the agent and pay the fee, or look for another buyer.

Eliminating the Points

For the buyer, the biggest cash closing costs are usually the points to get the mortgage. If you're getting a mortgage for $200,000 and you've agreed to pay 2.5 points, that's $5,000 out of your pocket. (One *point* equals 1 percent of the mortgage amount; and 2.5 points equals 2.5 percent of the mortgage amount.)

In the past there wasn't much you could to curb this expense. Today, however, with most lenders you can reduce or even eliminate the points by simply agreeing to pay a higher interest rate. Indeed, lenders use points as a device to enable them to offer you a loan at a rate lower than the prevailing market rate.

For example, say that the going interest rate is 7 percent. However, to appear competitive, the lender wants to offer a mortgage at 6.65 percent. To do that, however, would mean the lender would incur a loss on the loan (by lending below market). So the lender instead collects the money up front when he or she gives the mortgage by assessing points. The lender may charge 3 points, for example. Using a complicated calculation, it may turn out that 6.65 percent interest plus 3 points yield a 7 percent return to the lender.

As far as the lender is concerned, loaning money at 7 percent straight or at 6.65 percent plus 3 points comes out exactly the same. Thus, when you try to obtain a mortgage and the lender says it's 6.65 plus 3 points, why not ask, "How much is it with no points?"

The lender should be able to make a quick calculation and, in this case, say 7 percent. Thus by paying a slightly higher interest rate (along with slightly higher monthly payments), you can avoid having to pay cash up front in the form of points.

Dealing with the Title Insurance and Escrow Companies

The last biggest expenses in the closing costs are the fees that go to the title insurance and escrow companies.

In the past, these fees tended to be relatively small. However, in recent years some companies have jacked up their fees to incredible sizes. Today some companies are charging two and three times what they charged only a decade ago. Therefore, if you could cut these fees, you could save hundreds if not thousands of dollars on a transaction. There are two ways to cut them.

The first is to simply shop around. Title insurance and escrow companies compete for business, and their rates vary. Check out half a dozen in your area. You'll probably be astonished at the differences. Then, when you're making your deal, insist that the escrow and title insurance be handled through a company with a cheap rate. Once you explain, the other party to the deal should be happy to go along.

But the agent might not. Although *bundling of services* (through which the agent gets a kickback) is unethical, and in some cases illegal, many agents insist that both buyers and sellers use the escrow and title insurance company of their choice, sometimes one that is affiliated with their real estate company. They often use a very convincing argument that goes something like this. "I've been involved in hundreds of deals, and the only ones that went sour were those that didn't use this company. This is the only company in which the people are reliable, and you can count on them to do the job right."

Pretty convincing, isn't it? Furthermore, it might be true! Nevertheless, if you're cost conscious, you may be willing to take a chance on a company whose rates are half of those of the company that the agent is pushing.

Just remember, that it's up to you (and the other party) to decide on which escrow and title insurance to use. The agent can suggest, but cannot normally demand.

The second way to reduce the costs is to cut a deal with a particular escrow and title insurance company. After all, remember that you're an investor who's likely to bring in a lot of business. If you're there every six months to a year with another deal, particularly as the deals get more expensive, there's a lot of money to made by the company. So tell them that you'll deal with them exclusively. You'll bring all your purchases and sales to them *if* they will give you a special rate.

Don't think this type of arrangement is something new or unusual. Title insurance and escrow companies regularly offer reduced rates to

better customers. Even if you're just a consumer who happens to sell
a house within a year after you bought it, the company may cut a deal
of anywhere from 5 to 25 percent. If you're an investor who brings in
deals on a regular basis, you may be given a regular discount.

TIP

The reason the title insurance companies say they can
offer a reduced rate to a consumer who resells a home
shortly after buying it is that they don't have to conduct
a long search. They need to search the title only back
to the purchase, perhaps a few months. Hence, there's
less work and less cost. However, many title insurance
companies conduct a search only back to the preceding
transaction anyhow, so you have to wonder.

Transaction costs, strangely named "closing costs," take a big
piece out of every real estate transaction. The more you can knock
them down, the greater your profits.

7

Seven Techniques Used by Successful Investors

If you're just starting out investing in real estate, chances are one of the big questions you have is, What makes for success? What techniques do the big winners in the field use? What are the moves that will lead to a bright future in real estate for you?

Here are seven techniques that I've observed are used by most successful investors in real estate. If you practice them regularly, you will enhance your chances of joining that winning circle too.

1. Concentrate Your Efforts

Just as no one can be all things to all people, neither can an investor hope to be successful buying all kinds of properties in many different areas.

When you first decide to invest in real estate, the opportunities will seem unlimited. You can buy houses or condos, strip malls or apartment buildings, industrial properties or bare land. You can choose to invest in the mountains or near the coast, in downtown areas of major cities or in the suburbs, in rural areas or in farmland. You can buy new or resale or even build yourself. There's a type of real estate out there that will excite every interest.

What's important to understand, however, is that it's unlikely you'll be able to successfully invest in all of it. Rather, the best way to begin is to limit your scope and then concentrate on your area of choice until you become expert in it.

In real estate, as in most other fields, knowledge is king. If you have more knowledge than others, you'll be able to discern true bargains and avoid pitfalls while others go astray. And, of course, the way to gain that knowledge is to study hard and focus your attention.

Begin with Single-Family Homes

That's why I always suggest starting with single family owner-occupant homes. These are everywhere. They are easy to purchase and to rent out. And even if you guess wrong the first time, you're not likely to get badly hurt.

Further, as you buy your second, third, and more homes, you'll get to know how the real estate market, and in particular how the single-family home segment, operates. You'll become expert in evaluating these types of properties. You'll get a keen understanding of their financing. You'll be able to see in a home those features that could increase its value that its seller missed. In short, you'll develop a sense for identifying bargain property.

Of course, that doesn't mean that you're limited to single-family homes forever. It's just the best way to get your feet wet. Once you've gotten some experience, it's wise to dabble in as many different types of real estate as possible.

One very successful investor I know moved his family to a mountain community and began buying and selling ranch land. Over the course of a few years he became quite expert in the field, and he now controls many excellent ranch properties. Further, agents and other new investors consult with him before they make their own purchases!

Another successful investor I know decided to concentrate on duplexes—double-unit homes. She buys and sells these on a regular basis. She's identified virtually all of them in her area and knows many of the owners by name. They know to call on her when they want a quick sale. She actually makes a market in these properties on her own!

Similarly, other investors specialize in apartment houses, or industrial buildings, or in commercial centers. However, these people usually didn't start there. Rather, they started small and worked into it. Most started with single-family homes.

Stick to a Single Area

I also recommend that you raise a "farm." As explained elsewhere, this is a geographical area where you plan to buy *all* of your properties. It can be as small as a single neighborhood or as large as several cities. But what sets it apart is that you concentrate your efforts there, and not go afield.

By farming a single area, you get to know the neighborhoods, intimately. You know which are on the way up, which are stagnant, and which are declining. You even know the homes block by block. That means that when a potential investment property comes on the market, you don't need to waste time investigating schools and crime statistics, local governmental policies and homeowner association attitudes. You already know all this. Indeed, if you're really on your toes, you'll even be aware of previous sales and be able to tell what the home is worth within a few hundred dollars.

Further, you may have a specific location in mind. So you go door-to-door asking owners if they're interested in selling. In this fashion you can pick up homes even before they come onto the market and, sometimes, get real bargains in the process.

Of course, by concentrating your efforts in one area, you maximize your time and save needless expenses. You can be close if a rental needs a faucet fixed and not need to call out an expensive plumber. Or if you need to find a tenant, you can put the ad in the paper, field the calls, show the property, and rent it up—instead of paying 12 to 15 percent of your rental income on a property manager. If you want to sell a home, you can easily spend time sitting in it at an "open house" when you sell it as an FSBO. (See technique number 5 below.)

In short, concentrating your efforts in a single area is the efficient way to buy investment property.

2. Spend More Time Buying Than Selling (and Be Prepared to Lose Deals)

One of the keys to successful real estate investing is to buy right. In fact, some investors feel so strongly that they use the motto "You make your profits when you buy, not when you sell." By this they simply mean that the characteristics that make a property resell for a big profit are already built into the purchase. Buy the right property in the right location for the right price, and your sales success is certain. Buy wrong, and you'll spend a lot of your time trying to figure out how to dispose of the property without taking a loss.

Of course, that means that you'll need to become adroit at property analysis. It's easy to say "Buy right" but quite something else to know which property is right and how much to pay for it.

One of the hardest concepts for most new investors to accept is that they'll make many offers that fall through before they get a successful deal.

TIP

It's better to lose out on buying 10 overpriced properties than to buy one.

Suppose you find a house that you want to buy. The location is perfect. The home itself is ideally suited to be an investment. And you've determined the right price to pay, and it's only 8 percent less than the seller is asking. (If the asking price is $200,000, the offer is for $184,000.) How much sweeter and easier a deal could be it be?

So you make your offer, fully expecting the seller to accept. Only the seller is stubborn. She feels that the house is worth every penny she's asking, and she won't come down a dime. She won't even counteroffer!

Suddenly your perfect deal is in jeopardy. The house is right, but you can't get it for the right price. What do you do?

As in football, you punt. You move on.

The trouble is that many investors worry that they won't be able to find a better deal. They worry that maybe their own calculations are wrong. They worry that while they're trying to figure out what to do, someone else will come in with a better offer.

So you go back and change your original calculations. Okay, you figure, you can easily pay 2 percent more and still come out. So you send in a new offer 2 percent higher than the last ($190,000).

Only now the seller is emboldened. Here you're sending in a new offer without her even countering. You must desperately want the house. Why should she even think about coming down in price?! So she ignores your offer. What do you do now?

Remember football? You punt and move on.

But this is the perfect house! You'll never find another to match it. And besides, within a few years no matter what you pay, it will be worth more, and you'll make a profit. So you throw in the towel and offer the full price ($200,000), 8 percent more than you originally calculated the home is worth.

Of course, you'll get the deal (assuming the seller's ego hasn't blossomed to the point where she now wants *more* than the asking price!). But what kind of a deal do you have?

Certainly, over a very long period of time, you'll come out okay. (That's the beauty of real estate!) But during that time, you've lost money. You've paid 8 percent ($16,000) too much for that house. If you get into a financial bind and need to sell quickly, you'll lose money. If the property appreciates at a reasonable rate of 4 percent a year, it will take two years just for you to get back to market value, not counting transaction costs. It's the sort of move that an inexperienced consumer buying one house every decade or so would make. It's not the move of a successful investor.

In short, you bought wrong, and that imperiled your profits. What's worse, you may learn the wrong thing from your efforts. You may learn that in order to buy a house, it's not what you calculate it's worth that counts. It's what the seller is asking. You may continue on to buy more properties at inflated prices, ruining your profits as you go.

The moral of our little story is that when the seller is uncooperative, remember football and punt. Remember, there are more than 65 million homes in the country, and in any given year probably up to 10 percent of those are for sale. That's a huge inventory to choose from. There's no lack of opportunity. There is, however, often a lack of fortitude. Remember, you determine what makes a deal a good one. If it's not good, you don't need to buy into it.

Perhaps one more example will help. I recently was called on by a friend to help with the purchase of a home in a downtown area of Philadelphia. Since I wasn't familiar with the area, my advice was more a philosophical than a practical plan of operation.

Jerry called from Philadelphia and asked what he should do. He had made an offer of $300,000 on a house. The sellers were asking $360,000. They were apart by about 17 percent of the asking price.

The sellers had come down $10,000, and Jerry had gone up $20,000. The sellers then wanted $350,000. He had offered $320,000. The difference was $30,000, or about 8 percent of the original asking price. But they wouldn't budge. They countered his last offer by again offering $350,000.

TIP

A counter does not have to offer a lower price. It can simply reiterate a previous price, or the price could even be higher!

My initial response was to ask him what the problem was. Obviously this was not a deal made in heaven. There was a huge gap between what the sellers felt their house was worth and what Jerry felt was a good investor's price to pay. Simply move on, punt.

"But," Jerry said, "it's beautiful. It does need some work, but once it's put into shape, I should be able to rent it out easily. Of course, at the higher price I can't break even, even after taxes. But the area is only a few blocks from one of the top areas in town. It'll be real easy to resell.

"And it's beautiful. It's nearly a hundred years old, and the lines are just classic. I've always wanted to own such a beautiful house."

I thought a moment, then asked him if he had considered all of this when he made his original offer of $300,000.

"Of course I did," he answered haughtily.

I then asked him why he had increased his offer by $20,000. How had his figures changed?

Jerry stammered a bit and said he went back and recalculated. He figured that maybe he could squeeze out a few hundred dollars more in rent if he fixed it up really nicely. Also, maybe the comparables weren't in quite as good shape as this property would be when it was fixed up. In short, he figured he could come out with the higher $320,000 figure (which was still $30,000 less than the sellers were asking).

"Okay," I replied. "Then, from what you're telling me, it seems that it's quite safe for you to pay $300,000 for the home. On the other hand, if you're willing to take some risks and if everything goes just right, you might get away with paying $320,000 for the house. That's probably not the best way to buy, but just maybe you'll come out.

"But," I continued, "the sellers are in no way interested in the $320,000 price. They want $30,000 more. And from what you're saying, no way does the property warrant that much more money. So what's the problem? Simply punt, walk away."

"But," Jerry whined, "it's the sellers. They just don't see that their property is worth less. They simply won't listen to reason. Do you think if I came back at $325,000 ($5,000 more), they would see the light?"

Now I understood what the problem was. This was no longer an investment for Jerry; it was a love affair. He had fallen for the house, and in his emotional condition, no price was too much to pay for it. My final advice to him was to wait and see. "Why not give it some time," I suggested. "Don't do anything for a few weeks. Maybe by then the sellers will come around. In the meantime, why don't you keep your options open? Why not keep looking for other investment houses?" In other words, maybe in a few weeks your infatuation with the property will pass and reason will again take hold in your mind.

Jerry agreed. I got a call about a month later. No, the sellers of that original home hadn't come down in price. But he had found another property that was even better situated. He had made a low-ball offer, and after some countering, he had bought it at a good price. He still regretted missing out on his beautiful house, but his pocketbook was going to be fatter for having let it go.

The moral of the story is that in order to get a property at a price you want to pay, you may need to make offers on two, three, a dozen, even two dozen different properties. When the sellers don't go along, you remember football and punt. You move on to the next property.

In short, you simply play the numbers. There are a lot of good potential investments out there. If one doesn't pan out, keep making offers until you find one that does.

3. Identify the Neighborhood Loser—and Buy It

It's very rare for a good property to jump out and stare you in the face. But this does often happen in the form of the neighborhood loser. This is a property that because of some underlying factor, no one wants. And as a result, it's selling for considerably less than its neighbors.

It's helpful here to think of the word *crisis*. In Chinese it actually has two meanings: "danger" and "opportunity." The neighborhood loser is the same. It's a house that could be very dangerous to buy. Its detracting feature could prohibit it from going up in price and could make it difficult to resell. On the other hand, if you're creative and can identify and correct the detracting feature, you can almost overnight jump the property's value.

Okay, now that I have your interest, what do I mean by a "detracting feature"?

It could be anything from purple paint to being next to a large billboard. It could be a home that's too small or too large for its neighborhood. It could have no view in an area of view homes. What makes this property easy to identify, as I noted, is that it jumps out at you. Typically its price is far lower than its neighbors', and the problem is usually easy to see. It's a property that's crying out for attention.

A few years ago a neighborhood loser jumped in my face. I was looking in the East Bay area of San Francisco in a town near Walnut Creek. All the homes were tract built, but they were well designed with a custom look. They were expensive, at the time going in the $400,000s. All except this one house that was listed (but not selling) for $350,000. Why, I asked myself, and I went to see it.

From the street it seemed normal enough, except that it was slightly below road level. That means you looked down on it. This is not a desirable feature, but it is not in itself anything terrible, particularly since the drop was only a couple of feet.

However, when I went through the house and into the backyard, I immediately saw the problem. The house was literally in a hole. The homes on both sides and in back were on higher ground. That meant that the neighbors could literally look over their fences and down into the home's backyard. There was not even a semblance of privacy. And no one wanted to buy a home where they would be under a magnifying glass. All buyers had passed on the property.

I calculated that the house was selling for at least $50,000 less than its neighbors. I offered $325,000, and the sellers accepted without countering. They were thrilled to get out. I had bought the property for $75,000 less than its comparables, not counting the poor location.

But, you may be thinking to yourself, the one thing you can't change is location.

True, you can't move the house elsewhere. But sometimes you can disguise a location. Along one side I immediately planted quick-growing shade trees. When I bought them they were about 6 feet tall. When I sold the house two and a half years later, they were 12 feet tall, and they filled out to screen that neighbor's property.

TRAP

Beware of planting a *living fence* (trees along a property line). Some homeowners' associations and some conditions, covenants, and restrictions (CC&Rs) won't allow them over a certain height. Check first.

Along the back of the property—it had a deep lot—I planted several fruit trees. After a couple of years they not only shielded the property from the neighbor back there but they provided fruit as well—another positive.

On the final side, which was most closely to the level of my property, I got the neighbor to agree to a seven-foot instead of a five-foot fence and planted bougainvillea (a plant that grows quickly and tall, clings to fences, and provide beautiful flowers). Now that side was shielded too.

The final problem was caused by the fact that water runoff from the neighboring property all came through mine on its way to the street. That meant that my backyard was wet and puddling a large part of the year and that there was standing water under the house.

A *French drain* (which is essentially a pipe with holes in it placed underground) collected the lot water and moved it to the street. A sump pump under the house ensured that it remained dry.

When I went to sell the house, still in the same location, still in the same "hole," it did not look like it had any problem at all. Indeed, the backyard was a wonder of seclusion. It had beautiful flowers on one side, tall trees on another, and fruit-bearing trees in the back. It no longer was the neighborhood loser; it was a winner. And I got a good price for it, equal to comparable "well-located" neighborhood properties. Needless to say the profit was very satisfying.

The moral to this story is that when a neighborhood loser jumps up and stares you in the face, put on your creative cap. Begin thinking imaginatively. Try to discover if there isn't some way you can turn the situation into an opportunity.

In my case, careful landscaping was the key. In another case it may be repainting, or fixing a foundation, or roof, or . . . ? There are always neighborhood losers. What's really rare are investors who can see beyond the dangers posed to the profit potential.

4. Rent Relentlessly

As an investor in real estate, you will also inevitably become a landlord. You'll own property that you will need to rent out. When you first start, you may have only one or two rentals. However, after a few years you may have four or five, or even several dozen. With many properties, getting the rent in to cover your mortgage and other expenses is critical. Therefore, how you handle yourself as a landlord will determine to a large degree whether you'll be a success or failure in the field.

As a landlord, you will need to rent relentlessly. By this I do not mean that you'll be unfair—far from it. What I mean is that you'll be all business. You won't let personal feelings cloud the issue. And, as newcomers to the landlord market quickly discover, that's much harder to do than first appears.

I have a good friend, Joe, who's been in the investing-landlord business for nearly 30 years. Joe now owns close to 90 properties. Needless to say, he's quite wealthy. But, he still handles his rentals on his own. In fact, that's his full-time job. And it's really a pleasure to watch him at it. He's fair with his tenants—I've never heard any complain that he wasn't. But he's all business.

For example, he has a policy of no pets in most of his properties. He feels that pets leave odors, ruin rugs, and otherwise create high wear and tear. Therefore, he does not allow them in his best properties. (He does allow them in some of his properties that he says are his "dogs.")

I'm sure that there are many readers who have pets and who, indeed, love pets. I include myself in this group. As a landlord, you will have a choice to make—to allow pets or not. Your own experience will help you to determine how you want to handle it.

TIP

One way to help ensure that tenants who have pets take good care of the property is to charge a large pet deposit. Most good pet owners are happy to pay this, and in my experience, they leave the property in great shape when they move out.

Joe always asks prospective tenants if they have a pet. It's on his rental application form, and it is a question he puts to them directly. Most people answer truthfully if they do have a pet. Then he simply says he doesn't rent the property to tenants with pets.

Where his "all-business" attitude comes in is when the prospective tenants say something like, "Well, we really like the rental, so we'll get rid of our pet."

His standard reply is, "I would never rent to people who would get rid of their pet." It's hard for a pet owner rental applicant to argue with this.

When I asked him about this response, that he wouldn't rent to prospective tenants even if they agreed to get rid of their pet, he answered, "People don't get rid of their pets. When I was first in the business, I used to believe them. Then, I discovered that a few weeks or months into the rental term, the pet would reappear. A person who has a pet simply won't leave it behind. They just say they will to get the rental. So, I don't rent to them." That's his opinion.

By the way, it's important to understand that Joe has a pet terrier, named Charlie, which he loves. And he would never get rid of Charlie.

Joe also exhibits his business attitude when it comes time to collect the rent. If a tenant is more than a day or two late, he immediately goes to see that tenant in person. Unless it's an oversight, which it sometimes is, he insists that the rent be paid immediately.

TIP

Believe or not, sometimes some tenants will simply forget to pay the rent. These tenants need to be reminded. I generally will make it a point to stop by the first of each month for tenants who sometimes forget.

I have watched Joe in situations like this, and he is all business. While tenants sometimes don't have the rent, they always have an excuse—they had a medical emergency, or their relatives needed support, or they were late getting paid from their work, or they threw a terrific party with the rent money or . . . ?

Joe responds, "I understand you have problems, but the rent must come first. You will always need a roof over your head, and it won't be there if you don't pay your rent. No matter what your problem, you must pay the rent first."

He explains that he's found that people always have some money available in reserve. It's just a matter of priorities. If the landlord is willing to wait, they'll put something else first. But, if the landlord insists that he or she be paid first, then the rent becomes the number 1 priority and gets paid—on time.

Of course, if the tenants really cannot pay, then Joe insists that they move out. But, as I said, he's fair. I've seen him give tenants $500 to help them move when they were in a really distraught situation. On the other hand, I've seen him quickly go to court to get an *unlawful detainer action* (eviction) when tenants wouldn't cooperate or even discuss the problem with him.

Does Joe rent relentlessly? Yes, he makes sure that he always gets his rent, on time. If he didn't, he wouldn't own as many properties as he does, or be as wealthy as he is.

Is he unfair? I've never seen him to be. He provides good, clean properties at a fair rental price. He simply expects to be paid in return. If tenants have problems, he sympathizes, but he does not make their problems into his own by allowing late rent.

Will you, as a landlord, need to be as relentless as Joe?

Probably not. I find that I'm much more of a softy than he is. But then again, he owns a lot more properties than I do.

5. Sell and Buy on Your Own

When you're getting started, you definitely need all the help you can get. That includes the services of a good, experienced broker. However, once you've established yourself in real estate, you may want to consider handling deals on your own. The reason, as described in Chapter 6, is the high transaction cost, mainly the commission to the agent.

An agent's fee is usually 6 percent for residential property (as much as 10 percent for some investment properties such as apartment buildings, strip malls, and so on). If you can handle the transaction yourself, that could be money in your pocket. And it works both when buying and selling. When buying directly from the seller, you may get a price reduction for at least part (if not all) of what would otherwise be an agent's fee. When selling, there's no commission to pay if you don't use an agent.

However, it's important to understand that agents earn their fees. If you don't use an agent, *you* will have to do his or her work. That includes the following:

What You Must Do If You Don't Use an Agent

- When selling, advertise the property to find a buyer.
- When buying, scout to find a suitable property.
- Negotiate directly with the other party.
- Write up the purchase agreement.
- Handle all the paperwork.
- Open and manage the escrow accounts.
- Arrange for financing.
- Close the transaction.

It sounds like a lot. But once you're experienced with many deals under your belt, it will all seem doable. In fact, most experienced investors I know regularly scout out and buy properties at advantageous prices all on their own. Here's an example: Terry works with small apartment buildings, typically four to six units. These are often built as a group in certain neighborhoods, perhaps a dozen or even 30 at a time. Once he identifies a cluster of these small apartment buildings, he goes to the county assessor's office, and by looking at the public records, he identifies the owners.

TIP

The tax records for all real estate are in the public domain. If you're willing to spend the time, there's no reason you can't find the name and address of the owners of virtually any property.

Terry then calls the owners on the phone, identifies himself as an investor in real estate, gives them the address of their property, and asks if they've considered selling. Most owners are surprised to hear that Terry knows they own the property, and they often ask how he found them. He explains that it's not a secret.

Then many will simply say no, they're not interested in selling. But almost everyone will take down Terry's name and number and promise to call when they are ready. After all, sellers figure if they can sell directly to Terry, they can save themselves at least part of the commission!

Terry also keeps track of who he's called, and over time he builds up a database of owners. This is his "farm." At least once a year (and sometimes every six months), he calls back or sends a note, thus keeping in contact. And sure enough, he gets calls from sellers when they want to sell their small apartment buildings.

No, Terry doesn't buy from everyone who calls. Or even from every fourth one. Most sellers want too much for their properties. But every so often someone calls who wants to sell immediately, today, and is willing to offer a good price to do so. And Terry gets his good deals. When I last talked with him, he had over a dozen small apartment buildings and over 70 rental units, and his equity was high and growing.

Avoiding transaction costs is something you will want to grow into, as your expertise in real estate develops.

6. Hold for Market Highs (and the Art of Holding)

In this book we talk a lot about buying and selling real estate. In doing so, you may have gotten the impression that this is what successful investors do all the time, without regard for anything else. Nothing could be further from the truth. The savvy investor pays very close attention to both the overall financial condition of his or her area and the country, as well as the real estate market (and in particular whatever segment they are in).

TIP

The goal is to sell when the market is high and to buy when it is low. While this may seem obvious, determining highs and lows can be difficult.

In the residential market, investors were selling high-priced property after the turn of the century, when others were buying them. The reason was that prices had risen to historic highs, and the investors were sometimes selling for a 200 percent profit!

Of course, in order to sell, the investors had to have first purchased. These same investors had bought these properties during the severe real estate recession of the early 1990s. At that time prices had fallen by as much as a third of earlier values in many areas. Bargains galore were out there. And the savvy investors picked them up, rented out the properties, and held them until times got better.

As I said, it was an obvious move. But relatively few people actually did it. The reason was that in 1999–2002, when prices were shooting up, most people wanted to buy, hoping to resell at even higher prices. And in 1995–1997 when prices were collapsing, few wanted to buy for fear that prices would go even lower.

The truth of the matter is that most people buy and sell at just the wrong times, spurred on by the emotion of the market. A successful real estate investor, however, will put emotion aside and buy when prices are low, sell when they are high, and hold until the right time.

All of which is to say that while it's important to be in the market, it's equally important not to churn your properties. You don't want to sell just for the sake of selling.

Being able to wait out the real estate cycle until prices move up (eventually, prices will almost certainly move up in most real estate markets because of inflation and housing shortages) is, in fact, much of the key to success in real estate. However, being able to hold means that you must have stable properties.

This gets us back to the concept of the "breakeven." You will find that you can't hold onto a property with a serious negative cash flow. While you might grit your teeth and hang onto one or even two such properties, a dozen will quickly drive you to bankruptcy. Therefore, to reiterate, your goal should be to buy properties for which the income comes close to matching expenses—that is, those properties that you can sit on for years, if necessary, until prices go up and you can sell for a profit.

However, even the best investor sometimes buys a property that turns out to be a dog. No matter what he or she tries, the property loses money each month. When that happens, my philosophy is to "dump the dog."

If you have a property that can't be sold for a profit and that bleeds you with negative cash flow each month, sell it even if you have to take a loss. The reason: Once you're rid of the dog, you'll have a better outlook, probably will have more cash spendable, and you'll be able to move on.

Having a negative cash flow dims your perspective on real estate. You begin to think of the field as having few possibilities. And you stop looking for good deals. Indeed, I've known investors who've come to a complete halt simply because they bought into one bad property. The solution is to get rid of that property and move on. You'll find that the loss, which often turns out to be smaller than you'd thought, can be made up quickly by the next, better property.

The moral is simple: Sell when the market is high, and buy when the market is low. And dump the dog.

7. Keep Your Day Job

The best way to invest in real estate is to do it on the side and in your spare time. The reason is that you won't have much positive cash flow in the early years.

Yes, once you've been in the business for 20 years and have 10 or 20 properties that have gone up in value, with rents that have gone up similarly, you may indeed have significant cash flow. But until then, chances are you won't. That means that you need to have a steady source of income to count on.

Married investors often keep one spouse working full-time. In addition to maintaining a steady of flow of income, this also provides job benefits such as health insurance. As a real estate entrepreneur, you're on your own in terms of all the niceties that being an employee offers. That's why remaining employed is so consequential.

Many single investors keep their regular job full-time and work on their real estate investing in the evenings and on weekends. In fact, if you plan on doing nothing more than spending 5 or 10 hours a week on your real estate investments, you should thrive in the field.

On the other hand, the time you spend will probably not be at your convenience. When a good deal suddenly appears, you have to be "Johnny on the spot" to take advantage of it. That means being ready to make an offer any time—morning, afternoon, or evening.

And once you own property and become a landlord, you're going to be at the beck and call of your tenants. When there's a problem, you're the person they'll call. That could mean emergency calls at 2:00 in the morning to tell you about a leaking pipe.

Yes, it takes only a few hours a week. But those hours can be at very inconvenient times.

TIP

Not everyone should invest in real estate. It's a demanding business. You're on call 24/7. If you simply don't want to be bothered, if you want to reserve your weekends and your evenings exclusively for your own personal gratification, then do not invest in real estate. On the other hand, if you're willing to give up some personal time in the short run for long-term success, then by all means jump in.

Investing in real estate can be a no-brainer. It's a matter of simply acquiring properties one at a time until you're wealthy. You just have to make a few sacrifices, such as initially keeping your day job, to accomplish it.

Here, then, are the seven techniques that I have found almost all successful real estate investors use:

Seven Techniques Used by Successful Investors

1. Concentrate your efforts.
2. Spend more time buying than selling (and be prepared to lose deals).
3. Identify the neighborhood loser-and buy it!
4. Rent relentlessly.
5. Buy and sell on your own.
6. Hold for market highs.
7. Keep your day job.

8

Buying Apartment, Office, and Commercial Buildings

While I've stressed that the best place to get started investing in real estate is with single-family homes (they are the easiest to buy and you can simply ride the wave of their price appreciation), they are not your only options in real estate. Many investors graduate to other forms of profitable investment. In this chapter we'll look at two: apartment houses and commercial buildings.

Moving Up

Why move up? You could, as many real estate investors do, spend your entire career at the single-family home level, and as we've seen, you could do very well at it. But if you want to make more money and quicker, the answer can be larger properties.

For example, if you own a 20-unit apartment building or a 10-unit strip mall, you not only can expect to reap profits over time but, if you obtain the proper financing, you also may be able to obtain significant cash flow right from the beginning. In other words, you may be able to afford to hire someone to manage the property so you don't have to constantly be collecting rent and fixing broken dishwashers. Further, at the end of the month, you may have considerable money in your pocket over and above expenses. Plus, if you buy right and improve the properties, you may have significant and

rapid equity growth. Small wonder that many investors opt for the
bigger properties!

On the other hand, the potential for loss is also greater. If you
have only one rental house, you need to find only one tenant. Even
in hard times, you can always drop your rent a few dollars a month
and keep your property fully occupied.

With larger properties, you may need to find 10 or 20 tenants. In
tough times, you may be able to rent out only half or three-quarters
of your units, resulting in serious negative cash flow problems. In
short, you can lose a bigger property more quickly and more easily
than you can a single-family house. Thus, going big not only promis-
es greater rewards but also greater risks.

TIP

Investors in larger properties always seem to point out
that if they have one vacancy, only a fraction of their
overall rental income is affected—1 unit vacant out of 20
is only 5 percent of the total income. With a single-family house, 1 unit vacant represents 100 percent of your
rental income! What they fail to say is that they almost
always have 1 or more units vacant as a normal part of
tenant turnover, while a careful investor can keep a single-family home rented almost 100 percent of the time.

Making Profits on Large Buildings

It's important to always keep your eye on the donut and not on the
hole. Similarly, in investing, it's important to know where the profits
come from. For those who are intrepid, there are quicker and bigger profits to be made in larger properties. But that's because the
dynamics of the two fields are different.

Profits in Single-Family Homes

With single-family homes, prices go up only as overall residential
market values increase. If you buy with 10 percent down, for example, and the value of the property goes up by 10 percent, you've

made a 100 percent profit (forgetting transaction costs for the moment). Don't see it? Here's how it works: A house may cost $100,000. You put $10,000 into it, obtaining a 90 percent mortgage for $90,000.

Now, the value goes up 10 percent to $110,000. What's you're profit (in the form of increased equity)? Remember, your mortgage is $90,000. So your equity is now $20,000, twice what you started with for a 100 percent profit!

Profiting in Single-Family Homes

Down	$10,000	Equity	$10,000
Mortgage	90,000		
Purchase value	$100,000		
Increase	10,000	Equity increase	$10,000
New value	110,000	New equity	20,000
(100% profit)			

Of course, all of the increase in value of the property goes toward your equity. The lender does not share in any of it. You normally lock in the mortgage at a fixed amount, and any increase in value over that amount is yours! That's called *leveraging*, and it's one of the reasons that real estate is such an attractive investment.

However, there's a down side to this. If property values overall do not increase, then you make no profit at all. If your home continues to be worth $100,000, your profit is zero. If the value of the home should decline, your profits (equity) would go down just as fast.

Profits in Apartment Buildings

On the other hand, let's consider an apartment building. With an apartment house, prices are directly tied mainly to rental income. Simply increase your rents and you can produce significant profits overnight.

Further, the rental market does not always move at the same rate or in the same direction as the market for single-family homes. For example, in any given area, there may be a shortage of rental units but a strong supply of single-family homes. Thus rental rates can be going up at the same time that single-family home prices remain stagnant (or decline).

TIP

Until the housing shortage became acute in many parts of the country as we moved into the twenty-first century, the single-family-home market and the apartment market often worked in opposition to each other. When housing prices were going up, many people moved from apartments and bought houses (in order to take advantage of the potential profits to be made), leaving a surplus of rental units and depressing rental rates. On the other hand, when housing prices were level or declining, many people stayed in their apartment units, causing increased demand and increased rental rates. More recently, both markets have tended to move upward in tandem.

You may be wondering exactly how rental rates determine profits in apartment buildings. In theory, it's actually quite simple. For example, let's say you have a 10-unit building where each unit is rented for $500 a month, or $5,000 monthly, or $60,000 annually. The value of the property is based on that rental rate. Double the rental rate to $10,000 monthly, or $120,000 annually, and you've doubled the value of your building.

If you paid $500,000 for the building initially, double the rents and now you have a property worth $1,000,000. Keep in mind that this can happen while prices for single-family homes have moved up not at all. If you happened to put 20 percent down ($100,000) on your apartment building, your profit is now 500 percent (or $500,000)!

With apartment buildings, you can obtain magnitudes of profitability. Of course, as noted earlier, the risks are also great. If the rental rates were to fall in half, so too would the value of the building.

Profits in Commercial Buildings

Commercial buildings (as well as office buildings) operate in a similar way. Their value is directly determined by their rental income.

The greater the rental income, the greater the value. Buy a building at one level of rental income and increase rents, and you can sell at a higher price. (We'll go into this in more detail shortly.)

Another major factor in the financial aspects of owning commercial buildings (and industrial buildings too), however, is the strength of the tenant leases. Long-term leases with strong tenants (those likely to continue to pay their rent year after year with escalation clauses) mean a higher value. Short-term leases and weak tenants mean a lower value. Improve the leases, and you improve the value.

Additionally, there are other factors involved with these properties. For example, typically the rent for commercial buildings is determined by the *front foot.* Since access to the public is critical to businesses, the more exposure, the more valuable the location. Thus, a tenant will pay according to how many feet are directly accessible to the public as well as how good the location is.

TRAP

 In commercial buildings, the value of the property generally declines as the height goes up. For example, a commercial tenant on a second-floor mall generally pays less than a tenant on the street level of that same mall. The reason is that there's normally less foot traffic on the second floor—it's not as good a location.

If you can devise some way to increase access to the front footage, you can increase rentals. For example, opening the second floor of a mall to direct access from a parking garage can increase the value of the front footage of units in the building.

Profits in Office Buildings

In office buildings (or industrial buildings), on the other hand, access to the public is not usually a valuable factor. Thus, the front foot usually doesn't matter. For offices, the primary concern is the total amount of floor space. Thus, these buildings are rented out on the basis of square footage—so much per square foot per month.

This is the reason that office buildings can be built so high, even to the point of skyscrapers. The tenants often don't care what level they're at (as long as there are working elevators, of course!), as long as the rent is affordable. (Views from higher floors often command higher rents.) On the other hand, as we've seen, the higher you go, the less foot traffic, and, hence, the reason that commercial buildings (malls) are rarely if ever more than three stories tall.

Buying an Apartment Building for Profit

If you've a mind to purchase an apartment building, my suggestion is that you start out small—no more than 6 to 8 units. Also, I suggest you attempt this only after you have already purchased and rented out several single-family homes. (You will have developed your skills as a landlord in this fashion.)

When you approach an agent or seller of an apartment building, you will be advised that there are a number of methods of determining value. You can capitalize the net income, you can check comparables, or you can simply hire an appraiser.

However, the rule-of-thumb system called the *gross income multiplier* (GM or GIM) is often used by savvy investors to produce a quick and surprisingly accurate estimate of value, so we'll discuss it here.

Harry's Apartment Building

Harry had been investing in real estate for about five years, when he chanced upon what he considered a real opportunity. It was an eight-unit apartment building that the owner wanted to get rid of in the worst way. She was selling direct, FSBO, without an agent.

The owner, a widow in her seventies named Sheila, had owned the building for several decades. She had kept it fully occupied by always charging rents slightly lower than market. However, now Sheila was in ill health, and she wanted out, quickly. Harry saw an opportunity to jump in and get a bargain price.

TIP

Savvy landlords always charge slightly below market for rent in order to ensure their properties are rented up all the time. What they lose each month from charging a slightly lower rent is far less than they would lose if they waited with the property vacant for a month or two to get a tenant who would pay slightly more.

Harry asked around to several agents and learned that most were using a GM of around 10. That simply meant that they took the total rental income for a year and multiplied it by the number 10 to calculate the value of the property. The units were rented out for an average of $500 apiece, so the monthly gross (for eight units) was $4,000, and the annual gross was $48,000. When the GM of 10 was multiplied against this, it gave a value of $480,000 for the building.

When Harry asked where the GM number had come from, a real estate agent admitted she didn't know. Another said that it was simply a way of quickly quantifying the relationship between price and rental income in an area. For example, apartment buildings that were selling for around $500,000 were bringing in around $50,000 in gross annual rents. Hence, the GM of 10 was used. If prices moved up to $600,000 for buildings that grossed $50,000 in annual rents, then the GM would go up to 12. If prices moved down to $400,000 per $50,000 in rents, it would go down to 8.

Harry asked why prices would go up or down in relationship to rents, and she answered that the fluctuations were caused by the cycles of supply and demand. Sometimes more people wanted apartment buildings. Other times fewer wanted them and demand dropped. She admitted it also had to do with the cost of money and prevailing interest rates.

The agent asked if she could handle the transaction for Harry. But he declined, saying that he felt he was getting a good buy, and since the seller didn't want to use an agent, he was unwilling to pay for the service. The agent shook her head and wished him good luck.

TIP

Years ago a GM of 5 to 7 was common in many areas. Then, as investors began to see that they could buy apartment buildings, increase rents, and resell for substantial profits, the GMs moved up. At times, when conversion to condominiums was popular and highly profitable, GMs in the high teens were often used. It's important to understand that a second way an investor can make big profits in apartment buildings is to buy at one GM and resell at a higher one as times change.

The agent also pointed out that the GM could move up or down depending on the condition of the building. An apartment house in terrible shape usually commanded a lower GM than one in tip-top shape.

Harry conducted a survey of Sheila's building and discovered that there had been lots of deferred maintenance. The units had not been painted in years, and the carpeting was tattered. Also, many of the appliances were on their last legs. The tenants, however, were reluctant to complain because they were paying a rental rate that was below market.

In addition, the roof needed repairs, and the building overall looked shabby. It was in need of a complete paint job on the outside and an upgrading of the landscaping.

Harry went back to the agent and asked if a lower GM should apply because of the poor condition of the property. The agent shook her head. She said the demand for rental property was strong and Sheila's apartment house wasn't really that bad.

So Harry offered Sheila full price of $480,000. He agreed to put 20 percent down ($96,000—obtained from profits made on buying, renting, and selling single-family homes) and to attempt to get a mortgage for the balance from a bank. The purchase offer was, of course, contingent upon his getting financing.

Getting the loan, however, proved to be more difficult than Harry had anticipated. The banks complained that he had no previous experience with apartment buildings. Further, he was stretched thin already because of his other real estate holdings. In the end he obtained a 70 percent mortgage at an interest rate higher than the market rate, while Sheila carried back a second mortgage for 10 percent at the market rate.

TIP

A second mortgage by the seller is common in larger real estate purchases. Here the seller accepts a loan instead of cash. Sheila was happy to do this because she needed income as part of her retirement and she owned the building free and clear. She actually would have preferred to give Harry a bigger loan, but he refused. (He would have been smart to accept, since the interest rate she would have demanded for total financing would have been lower than that he was paying the bank!)

The sale took about 60 days to complete, and then Harry had the building. He had Sheila walk around and introduce him as the new landlord to each of the tenants. Then he was on his own.

His first big shock came when the very next month, three of the tenants told him they were moving out. It turned out that they were actually relatives of Sheila, and she had exaggerated the amount they were paying in rent. They were, in fact, paying only a fraction of the income Sheila had projected for them.

When Harry called Sheila about this, she agreed. She said that she had put them down for a "fair market rental rate" even though they were paying about less than half. "You can certainly rent it for what I said they were paying. I just credited them with half the rent because of 'debts' I owed them in the past."

Suddenly, Harry had a big rent-up problem.

TRAP

When buying apartment buildings, it's very important to verify who the tenants are and how much they are actually paying. It's not uncommon for prospective owners to ask to see actual check-receipts from tenants and bank deposits from the seller. This helps to avoid nasty surprises later on.

But his woes weren't over. As the old tenants moved out, they demanded their cleaning-security deposits back. They each claimed to have paid Sheila $1,000, and it was fully refundable when they left, provided that the apartments were left in reasonably clean shape, which they were.

Again, Harry called Sheila. She confirmed that she had the cleaning-security deposits but refused to turn them over. She said, "They weren't part of your purchase offer. You never mentioned them."

Harry had to agree that was true but said he never thought about it. She said she was sorry, but since it wasn't part of the sale, she considered these funds to be her money. Harry would have to pay back the cleaning-security deposits out of his own funds.

Harry had to dig deep to pay back the security deposits of the three moving tenants, and he was even more dismayed to learn that when the remaining five tenants eventually moved, he would have to pony up their deposits as well.

On the other hand, he realized that as soon as he rented out the apartments, he would be able to charge a cleaning deposit to the new tenants and that would help offset the drain on his cash.

TRAP

Cleaning-security deposits can be a big factor in the purchase of apartment buildings. Sometimes the deposits are actually bigger than the down payment! It's important to know exactly how much is involved, who has the money, and who owes it before making the purchase. Savvy buyers will often visit each tenant and ask to see their copy of the rental agreement to determine just what's involved, here.

Harry had to come up with cash and had three out of eight units immediately empty. It was a crisis. However, he remembered that a crisis not only was dangerous but it also offered opportunity. He borrowed money on his credit cards, and as soon as the old tenants moved out, he had their apartments repainted, put in new appliances and carpeting, and raised the rents. He also had the exterior of the building completely repainted, fixed the roof, and put in attractive landscaping. Then he asked $750 a month (a $250 increase).

Harry had done his homework, and he had learned about investigating rental rates from owning single-family homes. He had looked around carefully and discovered that apartments of the size he had were renting between $500 and $800 a month in his area, depending on condition. He fixed up the condition and moved from the bottom of the market range to near the top.

As soon as he got the empty apartments rented up, he announced to the remaining tenants that he was raising their rents $100 a month. He explained that as a new landlord he had higher mortgage payments to make than Sheila (who owned the building free and clear) and he had made improvements.

Three more tenants moved out over the next three months. Harry went in, refurbished their apartments as he had done with the other units where tenants moved out, and rented those for $750 apiece.

Within six months, Harry's monthly rental income had soared from $4,000 to $5,500. His gross annual income was $66,000, making the building worth $660,000 using a GM of 10. Of course, he had spent about $10,000 a unit fixing it up ($60,000), so his increased equity was actually only $100,000, nevertheless a handsome sum.

Harry figured that over time he would fix up the remaining rentals, increase the rent, and boost his equity even further.

In addition, the increased rental rate gave him a positive cash flow, allowing him to have money left over each month after paying for the mortgage, taxes, maintenance, and repairs.

Two years later, Harry had increased rents again until he was averaging $800 a month per unit, or $6,400 total. His annual gross was $76,800, giving his building a value of roughly $768,000.

However, when he went to talk with some agents, he discovered that they were now using a multiplier of 11. The market had gone up as more investors wanted apartment buildings. (Of course, the market can also go down.) Harry's apartment building was now worth $845,000. His equity had grown to $365,000, in just two years. Were he to sell, he would make a very handsome profit, indeed.

It's Not All Easy Street

From Harry's experience, we've seen what an investor can do with a modest purchase in an apartment building. It's important to understand, however, that we've glossed over many of the pitfalls of owning such property.

For example, Harry could have had serious tenant problems. He might have had tenants who not only refused to pay the rent but then refused to leave. He would have had to resort to an *unlawful-detainer action* in court (eviction) to get them out, and when they eventually moved, they might have left the place a mess, requiring heavy-duty refurbishing.

No, this doesn't happen all the time. And, if you're a scrupulous landlord who carefully qualifies tenants, it may never happen at all. But it is a risk.

Additionally, we've assumed that Harry was free to raise rents at will. This is not always the case. Many communities have some form of rent control through which they limit the size and frequency of rent increases.

Further, economic conditions were fairly stable for Harry, but that's not always the case. Sometimes, in economic downturns, a number of tenants may not be able to pay their rent nor can they move out, which can leave the apartment building owner with long-term rental headaches.

All of these things "could" happen. They are the risks assumed by an investor in apartment buildings. However, if you pay careful attention to the details of the business and you have a bit of luck, they won't happen and your profits will be significant.

Buying a Strip Mall for Profit

Henrietta also was an investor in real estate who cut her teeth on single-family homes. After a few years in the field, she wanted to move up, and she felt that commercial real estate was the ticket for her.

Henrietta looked around and quickly realized that the easiest way into the field was to purchase a *strip mall*. This type of property goes by many different names, but in general, it is basically a small shopping center of anywhere from three to a dozen stores located typically on the corner of a busy intersection. We're not talking about Wal-Mart or Macy's. Rather, these properties typically consist of small businesses such as a pizza parlor or a dry-cleaning business or even a convenience grocery store. These are relatively small properties with small businesses just right for the beginning small investor.

Henrietta contacted several agents and found one who specialized in small, commercial real estate. He showed her several properties, one of which appealed to her. It was a strip mall that had five stores. It was on a corner of an intersection that was fairly busy. There was a convenience store, a small Thai restaurant, a camera shop, and two vacancies.

TIP

Every commercial property needs an *anchor*. That's a business that will draw in customers to feed the associated businesses. In a large mall the anchor is typically a department store such as Macy's or Nordstrom's. In a small strip mall, it's typically a convenience food or liquor store, although it could be a major fast-food franchise such as McDonald's or Burger King. Without the anchor, the mall clientele will be limited since the other stores won't be strong enough to draw them in, and the entire mall will be at risk. Always determine the quality of the anchor when looking at commercial mall property.

The owner explained that the previous tenants had just moved out, and he didn't want to rent up the units, instead leaving it to the new owner to pick and choose whom he or she wanted for new tenants.

The agent said that the owner's explanation was baloney. The previous two tenants had gone out of business, and the owner simply hadn't been able to find any new tenants. The apparent reason was that the strip mall was short on parking. The restaurant needed parking for fairly long periods of time, while the convenience store and the camera shop needed lots of short-term parking. That left little to no parking for any other tenants and starved them of business. In short, the landlord couldn't justify the rent on a front-foot basis because there just wasn't enough customer traffic.

Henrietta asked how much the property was worth, and the agent explained that the value was related to the leases. He would have to evaluate the total value of the leases over time, the strength of the tenants (their ability to stay in business for the term of the leases), and the chances for rerenting to new tenants.

In addition, the type of lease would be important. In this case they were *net leases*, which meant that the tenants would pay for their own repairs, maintenance, and even the taxes. (These are sometimes referred to as *net, net*—or even, *net, net, net*—leases depending on how much of the costs the tenant bears.)

As it turned out, all the leases were for five years, and each had only one year left. The agent explained this was both good and bad. It was good in that Henrietta could now negotiate new leases, hopefully at better terms. It was bad in that the existing tenants might decide to move out, leaving her with more vacancies.

It turned out that the seller was asking $700,000 for the strip mall. Henrietta's rental income for the year (before mortgage expenses) would be about $100,000, providing she could get all of the units rented. However, with the two vacancies, her actual income would be closer to $75,000.

Henrietta asked about financing and was told that there was a $300,000 existing mortgage on the building that could be *wrapped*. When she asked what that meant, she was told that the owner was willing to give her another $350,000 second mortgage and wrap it around the first.

The agent explained that this would mean that Henrietta would pay on a $650,000 mortgage directly to the seller. The seller would then make the payments on the first and keep the balance of Henrietta's payment for himself, as due on the second.

The agent explained that this avoided having to obtain any new financing, which might be advantageous for Henrietta because she had no previous experience in commercial properties, which might make it difficult for her to obtain the necessary mortgage. She would, however, have to come up with $50,000 cash down. The agent said that in such transactions, small down payments were just as common as full cash deals.

TIP

Wraparounds, or *"wraps,"* are frequently used in commercial deals. They often combine two, three, or more mortgages into one big mortgage. They require lender approval, which can sometimes be obtained if the lender's loan-to-value ratio is low (it's a low mortgage when compared to price). The advantages are that the financing can be easier to obtain and it is often drawn up at a favorable interest rate.

Henrietta bought the strip mall. The first thing she did was remove a planter area that had helped separate the mall from the street. This resulted in five additional parking spaces.

Then she rerouted the strip mall traffic by making the driveway one way only. Prior to that, cars could enter from both streets—it was a corner lot. With the new one-way driveway, drivers would now have to enter from one side and exit the other. This accomplished two things: First, it allowed quicker and easier access to the stores from the parking lot, and second, it prevented cars from having to cross the busier street to enter the parking lot, a practice that had been tying up traffic at the intersection and making it more difficult and less desirable for potential customers to stop at the strip mall.

In addition, she had the parking area retarred and had new white parking lines painted on it. Also, she redesigned the parking lanes so that they would all go in the same direction, meaning people could get in and out more easily than they could in the past. Finally, she put up signs indicating that parking was limited to a maximum of 20 minutes in the lot.

TIP

One of the keys to success in any mall area is to make the shops compatible. They must all help draw in the same type of customer in order to thrive. If the customer types are in opposition, the businesses will suffer.

The convenience store owner and the camera shop applauded her moves since their customers rarely stayed more than 20 minutes. But the Thai restaurant owner was furious. He said he now had no parking for his customers because they typically stayed one to two hours for meals. Henrietta was sympathetic, but she told him she had read his lease, and it did not provide for specific term parking. His customers would have to park on the street.

The owner said he would leave. He would break his lease. She said she was sympathetic, and if he wanted to leave, she would agree to terminate the lease. He was out within two months.

Then Henrietta rented the restaurant space to a take-out deli kitchen, at a higher rent than the Thai restaurant had been paying. With parking available, the front foot rent seemed much more reasonable to tenants. She also quickly rented the remaining vacant units to a dry cleaners and a small video store. Now all of the tenants required only short-term parking, which was readily available.

At the end of the year, Henrietta negotiated rent increases with the convenience store owner and the camera shop owner. She insisted all her leases be for a minimum of five years with annual increases based on the tenant's sales as well as inflation. Since business was now up because of the parking solution, the tenants agreed.

Armed with her new leases, Henrietta went back to the agent, who calculated out the value of the property. Henrietta was now pulling in nearly $160,000 a year, and the longer term, stronger leases helped increase the value of the property. The agent said she could get well over a million for it, perhaps a million two or three.

Henrietta was successful because she accomplished for a commercial property what she had learned to do with single-family homes. She bought a property with an identified problem, cured that problem, and was able to increase rents. In so doing, she very quickly increased her equity in the property.

It's important to note that while we have seen how profits can be made, we have skimmed over certain aspects of purchasing a commercial property. For example, we haven't gone into detail on the actual pricing or leasing. The reason is that this is a fairly complicated procedure and involves not only evaluating leases (as noted) but also involves determining the *return on investment* (*cash on cash*), both of which are beyond the scope of this beginning book. If you're interested in buying commercial property, be sure to contact a real estate specialist who can give you a detailed evaluation of any property you are considering.

Looking for an Office Building

Jerry found what looked like a terrific real estate investment. It was an office building at the edge of an industrial park. The park was made up of light manufacturing businesses and offices.

The building that Jerry found stood alone on the corner of two streets, and it was distinctive in appearance. While all the other buildings were of cement construction, this one was of wood with cedar wood panels stained a dark color. It stood out and was quite attractive. Unfortunately, it was also in terrible shape. The owner had neglected repairs for half a decade. It was in desperate need of a new coat of wood stain, several of the windows needed replacing and the roof had some issues. Jerry figured he could quickly fix it up and increase its value.

The building was rented to two tenants, one on each of two floors. The top floor tenant was a telemarketing firm that had six months left on its lease. The bottom floor was rented to a music publishing company that had a very long 10-year lease, of which 4 years were yet to run.

Both were *net leases,* meaning that the tenants paid for all their utilities and maintenance (but not building repairs such as roof leaks). The tenants were also responsible for any property taxes attributable to their business.

Both leases were negotiated during the down cycle in real estate that occurred during the mid-1990s. At the time, the owner was desperate to find tenants, so he had offered a "sweetheart" deal. The rents were extremely low, in the neighborhood of a dollar per square foot. Since each floor was 1,000 square feet, the income from each tenant was $1,000 a month, or $1,000 total. At the time that Jerry was looking at the building, he was told that as a rule of thumb, a multiplier of 12 was used, meaning that the building itself was valued at roughly $290,000.

Note: The square foot costs vary enormously across the country. In San Francisco, for example, during the dot.com craze, values of up to $70 a foot or more were not uncommon. (That has more recently slipped to perhaps half that amount.) In some rural areas, values of as little as 50 cents a square foot are not uncommon.

TIP

The cost per square foot of office space is different in every area. It's determined by supply and demand. Thus, while space in Los Angeles may be tight and prices high, it could be plentiful in St. Louis and prices would be low. Or vice versa. Typically when prices are high, developers construct many new buildings. Often this results in an oversupply, which forces prices down. This halts construction until the existing oversupply is absorbed and prices go up again, restarting the cycle. Also, the office space market operates independently of the real estate residential market. It is more closely tuned to the health of the local economy.

Since the economy in the area had since turned up, Jerry figured the rents were extremely low for the current boom times. All he had to do was pick up the building, based on their low rents, wait out the tenants, and then re-lease to these or other tenants doubling (or more) the rent, in effect, doubling (or more) his building's value.

The owner, however, was savvy to how the market worked. He knew that the market had been low when he rented to his current tenants and that it was now high. He was well aware that he himself could double (or more) the currents rents as soon as their leases were up and thus increase his building's value. Accordingly, he was asking $600,000, close to twice what Jerry figured the building was worth based on current rents.

When Jerry pointed this out, the landlord said that the current tenants would be out in six months and four years, respectively. Then rents could be jacked up to levels that would warrant the price. He was basing his price on the future value of the building.

Jerry pointed out that setting the price in that way was unfair. No one could be expected to pay today what a building would be worth tomorrow. The seller said he didn't care; he wasn't in a hurry. He could wait. If someone came along who saw things his way, he'd sell. If not, he wouldn't. He wasn't willing to budge even a nickel.

Ultimately, Jerry passed on the building. He figured that the owner-seller was being unrealistic. However, that's the seller's prerogative.

TIP

If a seller is willing to wait, there's no question that he or she will ultimately get his or her price. What some sellers often overlook, however, is the fact that time is money.

The moral of this story is that Jerry came in too late in the office building cycle in his area. He should have bought the building several years earlier, when rents and prices were down.

Of course, you can't go back into the past. But you can wait for the future. As we noted, the office building market fluctuates, perhaps more than any other area of real estate. All Jerry needs to do is to wait a few years. (And perhaps concentrate on other types of real estate investing during that time.)

Eventually the office space market will inevitably get overbuilt. And that's the time he can jump in and buy at a bargain, perhaps even the very same building that he looked at.

We've looked at a variety of real estate investments that you may want to consider once you get your feet wet in single-family housing. The options we've described are apartment houses, commercial buildings, and office buildings. Just keep in mind, however, that these are specialized investments requiring expertise to evaluate, finance, and price. If it's your first time, you'd be wise to secure the aid of a real estate agent who specializes in the field.

9

Investing in Bare Land and Developing Properties

The basis of all real estate value is the land. In most cases price appreciation is attributable almost entirely to land. It's not the structure that goes up in value, it's the land underneath (remember: location, location, location!).

Because of its intrinsic worth, some real estate investors specialize just in land. In real estate terminology, those who buy bare land and then resell it for a profit without developing it are often called *speculators*. Those who buy bare land, build on it, and then sell are called *developers*. And those who buy broken-down buildings, scrape them off the land, and then build new structures are often *fixer-upper specialists* (usually *contractors*). In this chapter we'll consider these types of transactions and others.

Dealing in Single House Lots

Bare land is both the hardest and the easiest real estate investment to work with. There are many reasons for this. On the positive side are the following:

- You don't have to worry about tenants or collecting rent.
- Profits are often large.

- You can make deals with either cash or short-term (three years or less) seller-mortgages.
- Turnover can be quick, sometimes as short as a few months, if the market is with you.

On the other hand, it's not all a bed of roses. There are many risks involved in investing in bare land:

- It usually takes a lot of cash.
- Financing options are few if available at all.
- There may be many hidden pitfalls, difficult to uncover.
- It may take a long time to sell if the market turns against you.

Land speculation often involves buying tracts of land that are then developed. We'll consider this type of purchase in the next section. In this section we'll deal with a single lot that can be handled by a beginning investor.

Where are you likely to find lots? They are readily available in rural areas. Some can be found in suburban tracts where developers have overlooked parcels here and there. And a few, very few, are still available in urban settings.

Janet had gotten her feet wet investing in several homes, and now she wanted to expand her horizons. A few blocks down from one of the homes she owned was a vacant lot. It was the only vacant lot in the entire tract of homes, and when she walked by it, as she sometimes did on an evening stroll, she couldn't help wondering why it didn't have a house on it. So she decided to find out.

Janet contacted the local county assessor's office, and from tax records she got the name and address of the owner. Then, simply using information in the phone book, she called the owner of record. A gravelly voice answered the phone, and she explained she wanted to buy the lot on Travers Street.

The voice said he wasn't interested and hung up.

Most people would have been sufficiently turned off by this to give up. Indeed, that's probably what happened to other investors who tried a similar ploy. But Janet was determined. And she had the owner's address.

So she went to visit Hal in person.

Hal was in his seventies, and he lived alone in an old house in an older part of town. When Janet knocked on the door and asked if she could come in and talk about real estate, he said no at first, but then he relented and invited her in. He said that not many people came by to see him, just those same nuisances who called on the phone trying to sell him things.

He made coffee for them, and they talked. Janet said she had seen the lot and wondered why it was vacant in the middle of a housing tract.

Hal explained that he had originally owned all of the land as an avocado farm. But developers had come along and made him an offer he couldn't refuse, so he sold out. But he kept one lot, bigger than the rest and in the best location, so he could eventually build a new home there. However, his wife died soon after that, and he no longer had any interest in building.

Janet asked if would sell it.

Hal shook his head. He said he'd had many offers, but he had always refused. Then he looked slyly at Janet and asked how much she was willing to pay.

She said she had tried checking the comps, but there were no previous lot sales nearby. So, she had checked the assessed value of homes that had recently sold in the area. Their value was broken down between the cost of the building and the cost of the land. She said she'd pay what the assessor said the land in similar properties was worth, or what the assessor said his lot was worth.

"It's worth much more than that," Hal fumed. "Those assessors always knock the land's value."

"Nevertheless," Janet said, "I believe it's a fair price, and that's what I'll pay."

"Are you sure you want it?" Hal asked.

When Janet nodded, he said that he was probably too old to ever build on it anyway, and he'd think on it. When Janet called him back the next day, he agreed to sell.

Janet ran a quick escrow and secured title insurance, to be sure that title was clear and that Hal did, in fact, own the property. She discovered there was an existing road tax on the property for $450, which Hal agreed to pay off. Then she bought it. And then her troubles started.

She had in mind to either resell quickly to a builder (good land was scarce in her suburb) or to actually build a spec (speculation) home on the property herself. For her to build on the lot herself, the lot would have to be truly buildable, meaning it had to have utilities. Janet quickly discovered that utilities, though in the street, had never been connected to the property. Before the lot was truly buildable, she'd have to connect to power, water, gas, and sewer lines. There were fees for each connection, and the total was close to $10,000! Plus, to secure a building permit, the local school district required a donation of 5 percent of her estimated building costs to go toward new school construction. On a $200,000 house that was another $10,000. And all of it was cash.

She immediately gave up her plans for building on the lot herself and instead contacted several contractors. They were all interested. However, they would encounter the same costs as Janet. So when they made their offers, the offers were reduced by the costs of utility connections and school donations.

Nevertheless, the land was valuable, and when the top bid was in, Janet saw that she could sell the lot for significantly more than she had paid for it. She did sell it, and she pocketed her profits (after putting aside enough to pay her income taxes).

There are four morals here. The first is that you should never believe what the county assessor says a property's land value is. Very often these assessments are only a fraction of the real market value. In California (and other states), for example, assessments are made upon sale and not significantly updated, even when prices increase. In other states, assessments can be as much as 10 years or more behind the market. You should check it out yourself.

Second, an overlooked lot in a built-out development can be very valuable. The lot's true value is based not on what the land originally sold for when the area was an agricultural field but on what it will be worth when it's developed. When the lot comes up for sale, contractors will often bid on the opportunity to get it and calculate their profit from the combined home and lot.

Third, you must always thoroughly check out bare land for utilities and other hookups. Janet was lucky in that they were nearby in the street. But in the case of rural land, it might have been necessary to have the hookups dragged for hundreds of feet, sometimes miles, which would have cost far more than she could pay.

Finally, you never know if someone will sell until you ask. A word of caution, however. When dealing with elderly people, be sure they are competent to enter into the transaction. Else, later on, a relative or other interested party could say you used "undue influence" to coerce them into signing and attempt to rescind the deal.

TIP

When you buy bare land, you must also check out the land itself. For example:

- Will the ground support a house, or is it too swampy?
- Is the ground loaded with boulders requiring expensive blasting?
- Does the land drain, or is expensive drainage required?
- Are there lots of trees that need to be felled, costing a load of money?

For more information on buying lots, check into my recent book *Tips & Traps When Building Your Own Home,* McGraw-Hill, 2001.

Land speculation is like any other type of speculation in a commodity from gold to soybeans to stock and bonds. If you guess right, you can make a killing. If you guess wrong, you can get killed.

Changing the Land's Use

The biggest profits I've seen in land speculation have come about when land was converted from one use to another. For example, I have seen tremendous profits made when undeveloped land was bought and then resold later as prime industrial or residential lots. Initially, the land was worth a few thousand dollars an acre to the farmers who owned it, but, as developed land, it became many times more valuable. Of course, there are significant impediments to getting the land use changed, as Marc would find out.

Like Janet, Marc had started out investing in residential housing, and as he acquired more experience, he wanted to move onto something bigger and better. So he began checking around his city until he found a parcel of about three acres. (An acre is 43,560 square feet, which in many communities roughly equals the size of five or six typical residential tract lots.) The land had been used for vegetable farming, but in recent years with homes built all around, it had been allowed to grow fallow. Now it was nothing but weeds. The nearby homes, however, were selling in the $350,000 price range.

Marc contacted the owners, farmers who owned several other parcels of land, and they agreed to sell the parcel for $50,000 an acre, or $150,000 for the three acres—a price that was about four times what the land was worth as agricultural property. Marc gave them $10,000 cash in exchange for a two-year option to buy.

TRAP

An *option* gives Marc the right but not the obligation to buy the property. In this case the price was spelled out and the option money was to be included in the price. If Marc did not exercise his option within the two-year period, he'd lose his $10,000.

Next Marc went before the local planning commission and asked to have the land use changed from agricultural to single-family residential. However, before he made his appeal, he did his homework.

He did an evaluation of all surrounding property to show that it was mostly residential. He also took a petition around to the nearby neighbors to sign that they approved of the development. Some of the neighbors objected because they had hoped the area would be developed as a park. Marc pointed out that it simply was too small for a park, but that nice homes would get rid of the dust and blighted look of the open field. Most neighbors signed. More importantly, there was no open opposition.

TRAP

Getting a change of land use requires approval of a county or city planning commission. Any opposition from neighbors, particularly if it is large and organized, will almost certainly doom the effort.

Marc also got an architect to create a rendering showing how streets could be put in, and he got approvals from the local utilities and sewer district for eventual connections. He proposed four lots per acre plus, of course, wide streets and sidewalks.

It took the better part of six months, but eventually approval was granted. Now Marc had to go to the state. In order to subdivide land into twelve lots (four per acre for three acres), approval from a state real estate department (or commission) is usually required. This normally takes the form of getting subdivision approval.

TRAP

Some states have passed what is sometimes called a *subdivision map act.* The purpose of this type of law in most cases is to prevent fraudulent division of land where property lines are inaccurate or no streets or roads or utilities are provided or where title to the land is not clearly held.

Marc learned that his request would be filed in a queue in which it would sit until other land developers who had already filed their subdivision maps were processed. He was told that the procedure could last as much as a year or more. Further, there was all sorts of documentation required, and in order to get it right, he would need to engage an attorney who specialized in subdivisions.

Marc began to think he had bitten off more than he could chew. So he contacted a couple of experienced builders and asked if they would like to partner with him. They said that they didn't do such partnerships, but one offered to buy the land directly from him, for $75,000 an acre. That would give Marc a $75,000 profit on three acres. Of course, he would get only paper (a second or other inferior mortgage) initially—the cash would come much later after the land was subdivided and the homes were built and eventually sold.

Then Marc learned about a quirk in the law. In his state, a subdivision map was required *only* if the land was to be subdivided into more than four lots. If he subdivided it into just three lots, no such filing was required.

So he offered the property up for sale in one-acre parcels, zoned for residential use with four lots per acre. Small builders jumped at the chance to get good residential land in a prime area, and he soon sold the lots off for $100,000 apiece (total $300,000 or a $150,000 profit on three acres), part cash and part paper. (As part of the transactions, he bought the land from farmers by exercising his option, which he then sold to the contractors, all through the same escrow process.) Of course, now it was up to the contractors to get a subdivision filed, or perhaps, to build only three homes per acre.

TRAP

Care must be used when avoiding a subdivision filing by going under the minimum lot requirement. If the land is divided under the minimum and then again divided, the state may rule that an actual subdivision occurred that required filing. A total change of ownership and sales to different parties can help avoid this problem. Be sure you check with an attorney who specializes in this field first, however.

Marc realized a substantial profit for his efforts. And he did so in less than a year.

Splitting Land into Smaller Lots

Another way to make money in real estate is to increase the size of the pie. Where there is only one lot, make two.

Marcie did just this. After a careful search, she found an older house on a hillside located just outside the city limits of her town. The house itself was sitting on an acre of land. It was positioned to the front of the plot, near the street. Fully half the remaining land was open space behind the house, where the owner had planted fruit-bearing trees.

It was an exclusive area of town, and the property was for sale for $400,000. Nearby homes on half-acre lots sold for about as much. This house had the added advantage of the bigger lot, but on the negative side, it was old and run down, balancing things out.

The sellers were a middle-aged couple who owned their own business. They were relocating to a different state. Marcie tried to negotiate the price down, but they were adamant, so she eventually paid full price.

TIP

If you're getting a good deal, even full price is not too much to pay.

Marcie arranged for 90 percent financing and bought the property. Immediately after the purchase, she had the lot surveyed, isolated the back half acre, and dedicated a strip of land up the side to the street. She now had two lots: the front lot on which there was the house and the back, or *flag lot*, with its own access to the world.

She advertised the back lot for sale at $200,000. It only took a few months to find a buyer who was willing to pay $175,000 in cash. She thought she had everything licked, until she tried to close escrow on the deal.

Marcie discovered that the lender who had given her the loan on the property when she bought it had the entire property listed as collateral. The lender was not willing to give up even an inch of land and dilute its collateral. Marcie begged and pleaded, to no avail.

So she tried an end run. She had the property refinanced. This required a new escrow and title insurance. However, as part of the refinancing, she had the property lines redrawn reflecting the split-off of the back lot. She offered the new lender only the lot on which the house stood.

Since the house was on its own lot with nearly half an acre of land, the lender did not object. She got new financing, separated off the back lot, and sold it for $150,000 in cash.

Then Marcie fixed up the house and resold it for $450,000. Her total profit on the land split was $200,000

The moral here is that where there's a will, there's a way. The biggest problem with splits tends to be the lenders, who almost never will agree to reduce their collateral. Thus, you'll have to get new financing on each side of the split (or on only one side, as was the case here).

It's worth noting that splits come in many different flavors. In San Francisco, for example, where land is very pricy, I've seen clever investors buy flats (buildings where each floor is a separate unit) and split them condo style for big profits. In other cases I've seen investors split lots and buildings on them into duplexes or triplexes (where the structure would allow it).

The whole idea of the split is to create two (or more) parcels where previously there was only one. And in the process, of course, make a profit.

Scraping Land Purchases

The final land purchase we'll consider is the *scraper*. This refers to a property where the land is very expensive and the building isn't. Thus the building is "scraped" off the land, and a new, more appropriate one put up.

Scrapers tend to occur primarily in older areas where prices have gone through the roof. For example, in parts of the San Fernando valley of Los Angeles, scrapers have become common. Here, older, smaller tract homes, sometimes having only 1,000 square feet, were built on very large lots, sometimes a third to half an acre. This was the way it was done back in the 1950s when land was cheap.

These homes (and their lots) originally sold for under $12,000. Today, however, nearby newer and much larger homes on the same size lots are selling for well into a million dollars. Hence, the opportunity.

Stephen also had gotten his start in real estate in single-family homes. However, his specialty had quickly developed into fixer-uppers. He looked for run-down homes that he could fix up and then resell at a profit.

While searching, he came across the house on Maple Street. It was a typical tract home for the area—50 years old, run down, but on a huge third acre lot. And surrounding homes had been scraped with newer mansionlike buildings erected in their place.

The seller was asking $450,000 for the property. To Stephen, that seemed like an exorbitant price for a run-down, 1,000-square-foot house. However, the seller also realized that the value was in the location and the lot, not the house.

However, the seller was hamstrung by the house. It was on the lot, and instead of adding value, it actually detracted. Most buyers simply wouldn't consider it as a place to live, at the listed price. On the other hand, they weren't willing to undertake the task of knocking it down and starting from scratch.

Stephen, however, had the entrepreneurial spirit. He negotiated and eventually got the house for close to $400,000.

Then he had an architect draw up plans for a 3,200-square-foot "mansion." He got the plans approved by the city and hired a builder to do the work.

It took less than a day to scrape the old house. However, its connections to city sewer and utilities were saved (saving Stephen some additional hookup costs).

The construction took four months, and when it was finished the new building had cost him $425,000. He had $825,000 into the deal. Now he offered the property for sale at $1.3 million. And he got no offers.

The real estate market had taken another of its cyclical dips, and high-end buyers were few and far between. The house sat on the market for five months (with Stephen making huge mortgage payments) until he finally unloaded it for $975,000.

He did make nearly $75,000 after expenses; however, he could have made far more if the market had not turned. And in the meantime, he had many sleepless nights wondering if he would come out okay at all.

Scrapers are one of the scariest types of land deals to handle. They are best done by those who are already in the building trades. Contractors can save costs and handle construction for far less than an investor, who has to hire it out. Thus, a contractor's margins are lower.

In good times, scrapers can be wonderful investments, and I've seen investors rake in huge profits on them. But if the market turns sour or costs are too high, it's also very easy to lose.

Land investments are great and are one of the many different types of investments you may eventually want to try your hand at. Just remember, however, that they are usually for those who already have had some experience in the field.

10

Flipping Properties

Whenever I hear the term *flipping,* I'm always reminded of a fish out of water. However, flipping has nothing to do with fishing. Rather, it's a term that came about because it characterizes the rapid turnover of a property, *flipping ownership.* It means selling a property right after buying it. Indeed, it can mean never really taking title but instead making a profit by tying up the property and then quickly dumping it.

Flipping becomes fashionable mainly when there's a hot market. When properties are jumping up in value by rates of 10, 15, sometimes 25 percent a year or more, it's fairly easy to lock in a price and then resell for a higher price in very short order.

For example, you may buy a house for $150,000 and in a hot market, be able to quickly resell it for $175,000. If you're careful about how you do this and avoid most of the transaction costs, you can pocket a quick $25,000. In some cases, of course, the profit can be substantially more.

On the other hand, in a more normal market with perhaps 5 percent price appreciation annually, flipping is more difficult. It's much harder to find a property for which the price will go up so rapidly that a flip is justified. But for savvy investors who spend time looking, bargain-priced properties are available, and flipping these does make sense.

In a cold market, it's very hard to find a flippable property. With prices declining, it's simply very unusual to find a buyer who is willing to pay more than you did. Indeed, most buyers want to pay less.

What Are the Rules for
Flipping Properties?

To flip real estate, you need to follow certain rules. These rules are
not hard and fast, but if you break them you could suffer:

Rule 1: Buy low. The only way you can gainfully flip a property is to
pay less for it than market price, or buy at market and wait for values to rise. You cannot make money by paying over market for
properties or buying ones that do not quickly go up in value.

Rule 2: Lock in the low price. By locking in a price, you can resell for
a higher price. If you don't lock in a price, then the seller can easily sell to the next person and make the profit himself or herself.

Rule 3: Have your rebuyer ready. A *rebuyer* is the person who buys the
property from you. Since time is of the essence in these deals, you
can't lock up a property and then go out looking for a rebuyer.
You must have one who is ready to act.

And that's how it's done! No, not really, as we'll quickly see. But
those three rules form the basics. Of course, there is one other con-
sideration, and that's to keep yourself out of trouble while you're
flipping. You do this through full disclosure. You let all parties know
what's happening. That way there's less chance someone will come
back later on and say he or she didn't know what was going on and,
hence, was cheated.

What about Flipping New
Homes?

Have you ever seen lines of people waiting outside the sales office
when new homes go up for sale?

This happens when the market is hot and there are shortages of
homes. Did you think that all of those people were waiting in line to
buy a home to live in? If you did, you were mistaken.

Many of the people who wait in long lines to buy new homes are
hoping to flip the property. If there are 20 new homes being built
and the demand is for 500 (as has been the case in some areas over
recent years), that means that 480 people are not going to get a *new*
home. If you're one of the lucky 20, you can quickly sell to one of
the unlucky others.

Indeed, sometimes people will even sell a good place in line (if it's close to the front) for hundreds or thousands of dollars! To cut down on this practice, some builders have taken to getting the names of people in line. However, it's usually easy enough to say that the person whose name is on the list was simply a place-holder for the new buyer who takes his or her place.

What about Flipping Resales?

Savvy investors are always on the lookout for properties that are for sale at below market. If they find them, they tie them up and then quickly resell them. Sometimes the sales are from foreclosures, or REOs or probates or just from sellers who want out quickly and are willing to take less.

What Are the Steps in Flipping a Property?

It's really not that hard to do. The key is to lock in the price. Once you locate a property that's below market, you present an offer that ties up the seller. If the seller accepts, you have a period of time in which to resell, depending on how that offer was structured. Your time period can be anywhere from a minimum of about 30 days to a maximum of about six months.

TIP

The simplest way to handle a flip is to never take title yourself. The mechanics of doing that, however, can be fairly complex. However, the advantage is that you don't obtain a mortgage, so you don't need to qualify or pay mortgage costs.

You then bring in your rebuyer (one who actually purchases the property), who concludes the sale with the original seller. The money transfer is all done in escrow. The new buyer gets a mortgage and puts up a cash down payment in the usual fashion. A portion of the purchase price goes to cash out the original seller. And you get the difference, usually in cash but sometimes in the form of a second mortgage, for yourself.

There are two methods of accomplishing this: assignment and options. The option is the easiest to understand.

How Do I Get an Option?

Real estate options are not much different from stock options. For the buyer, they are an opportunity (but not a requirement) to purchase for a set price by some future date. For the seller, they are a commitment to sell usually for a set price by a set date.

The basics of an option are fairly straightforward. First you locate the property and make an option offer. If the sellers accept, you next give them option money (perhaps $1,000 at minimum) and they in exchange give you the right to purchase the property usually at a fixed price for up to a certain amount of time, typically no more than six months or a year.

Next, you find a rebuyer, someone who will purchase the property from you at a higher price. This is the person whom you, hopefully, have ready to go.

Finally, you exercise the option at the low fixed price agreed upon by the seller, and then sell to the rebuyer at the new higher price, keeping the difference, which is the profit. In actual practice, all of these moves are made simultaneously, and the seller pays the normal seller's closing costs and the rebuyer pays the normal buyer's closing costs with very few transaction costs left for you to pay.

And it really is that simple. The key, of course, is finding the right-priced property, the right seller, and the right rebuyer.

TIP

In an option, you the buyer are not committed to purchase. It's at your discretion. The seller, however, is committed to sell usually at a fixed price. He or she must go through with the transaction, *if* you execute your option.

The right property is one that is either undervalued or in an area where prices are accelerating. Check Chapter 2 for tips on finding these.

The right seller is usually someone who wants to get out and is strapped for immediate cash. Remember, in order to get an option, you pay the seller some money. It can be any amount, but it has to be enough to persuade him or her to give you an option. A typical amount might be between $500 and $5,000, depending on the value of the property.

The biggest problem with the option is the time factor. The term of the option is negotiable. Usually options run from 30 days to six months, but they can be for virtually any length of time. The trouble is that sellers usually want out quickly, and a seller who is willing to give you an option of more than 60 days is unlikely to be willing to also give you a good price.

In the past, options in real estate were used primarily for properties other than residential. They were used to buy land, commercial or industrial buildings, farms, and so on. They were used to allow the buyer time to obtain difficult financing, for example, or to secure a change in zoning, or for some other similar reason.

Recently, however, they have been increasingly used in residential real estate as part of a flipping strategy. In these cases the time frame is typically very short, less than three months, and the amount of option money given to the seller is likewise usually small, typically under $5,000.

TIP

Remember, the key to flipping (using the option) is to have a rebuyer waiting and ready to go. If you have that rebuyer ready, you can handle a transaction easily in 60 days. Indeed, you can handle it in 30 days, or perhaps even less. But, if you have to go out and find a rebuyer once you have the option, time puts a stranglehold on your potential success in the deal.

How Do I Handle the Paperwork for an Option?

You can get an option document at most stationery stores or legal supply houses. However, you should take it to an attorney who will rewrite portions of it to suit your specific deal. This is what the seller will sign to give you the option.

When it comes time to exercise the option, you simply open escrow as if you were going to buy the property. However, your rebuyer does all the qualifying for the mortgage and puts up all the down payment and normal closing costs.

When the deal is ready to close, your option is exercised. For a moment you own the property, but then it is transferred to the rebuyer. It is all handled in escrow.

Note: while an option is not complicated, there is plenty of room to make a mistake. Therefore, certainly the first time you use it you should have someone experienced, such as a good agent or attorney, lead you through it. Yes, that will cost more, but in the long run it can save you a lot of headaches (and possibly money).

TIP

It's important that you disclose to the rebuyer the amount you are actually paying for the property. This avoids hard feelings and helps protect you from that rebuyer's coming back later and saying he or she was cheated. It's also a good idea to let the seller know, although with a valid option, it's really none of the seller's business what you do with the property after you purchase it.

How Do I Assign a Property?

Another way to tie up the property without buying it is to use an *assignment of purchase.* In this type of arrangement, you make an offer to purchase, usually for cash. However, when you make your offer, you state that the buyer is your name "or assigns." What this means is that either you can buy the property, or someone else to whom you have assigned the contract can buy the property.

Later on, you have your rebuyer step in, and you assign the purchase contract to him or her. Your rebuyer actually gets the financing and makes the purchase. And you pocket the difference between what you paid for the property and a higher price that the rebuyer pays.

Getting a seller to agree to an assignment, however, can be tricky. Some sellers won't go along with an "or-assigns" sales contract. The reason is that they don't know who will eventually purchase the property. They are afraid that you might not be able to get a needed mortgage and want a back door out, or that you're planning to sell your contract to someone else (which is, in fact, the case!) and that person may not qualify for a needed mortgage. In order to calm the seller's fears, you may need to put up a bigger deposit, or avoid putting many escape clauses into the contract, which can increase your risks.

Unlike the option, the ability to assign the contract runs only as long as the purchase contract is in effect, typically 30 to 45 days. That means that you've got to find a buyer and conclude your other end of the deal very quickly.

Hopefully you have done your homework and have a rebuyer waiting in the wings. This person picks up the assignment and actually moves forward with the purchase of the property. Again, you never actually make the purchase. The transaction is basically handled in escrow. At the end of the deal, you get your money out, typically in cash. The advantages of assignment are the following:

- You don't need to put in your own cash. You have to put up only the original deposit when you buy the property from the seller, and you get this deposit back from your rebuyer.

- You can expect to get your profit out within 30 to 45 days.

- You don't have to qualify to obtain a mortgage.

Of course, it's not all a bed of roses. There are some risks. You actually do commit to purchasing the property. To protect yourself from having to complete the purchase in case you can't find a rebuyer (or your rebuyer falls through), you'll want escape clauses. But escape clauses weaken your offer and lessen your chances of getting it accepted. So to make the deal, you may not be able to include many (or any) and have to take a big risk.

Assignments have been used in real estate for a long time. However, as noted above, you need to include lots of escape clauses in the deal in case you can't find a buyer in the short amount of time that you have, or in case that buyer, for some reason, can't complete the purchase.

How Do I Include Escape Clauses?

Escape clause? What's that?

An *escape clause* is one that says the sale and purchase are "subject to" or "contingent upon" something. If that something happens, you can gracefully (without financial harm) back out of the deal. In modern transactions there are three widely accepted escape clauses that most sellers will agree to without blinking:

1. *Disclosure contingency.* You must approve the seller's disclosures. If you don't approve them, there's no deal. But the time limit here is very short. In California, for example, it is statutorily three days. And if the sellers disclose nothing wrong, it's awkward to disapprove the deal.

2. *Professional inspection.* You get to approve a professional inspector's report. Don't approve it, there's no deal. Usually you have 14 days to get the report and then either approve or disapprove it, and if there's nothing wrong with the property, it's hard to disapprove of the report.

3. *Finance contingency.* You have written into the contract that the deal is contingent upon your getting financing. No financing, no deal, and you're out without penalty. This usually runs for 30 days, but you must reasonably look for financing.

Note: the language for these contingencies must be appropriate for your state and locale. Therefore, at least until you learn how it's done, you need to have a good agent or attorney write them in for you. The problem with these contingencies is that they probably don't offer you enough protection if you're making an assignment. They are for short periods of time, and they may not apply in your case. For example, in order to get the deal at a cut-rate price, you may have to offer the seller cash. In a cash sale, you don't have the protection of a finance contingency.

You might rely on the disclosure or the professional inspection contingency, but those usually run out after 14 days max. (And if there's nothing untoward about the property, you would be hard pressed to exercise them.) Once they run out, you either agree to move forward without their protection, or you back out of the deal.

If you agree to move forward and something adverse happens (your rebuyer peters out), you're stuck for the house!

As a result, most investors who are flipping using an assignment want to add other contingencies. These contingencies are easy to add but not easy to get accepted by the seller.

You can make the sale contingent on anything: your uncle's dying and giving you an inheritance, your great aunt's coming from Greece to approve the deal, sun spots, anything at all. However, any contingency you add that is not reasonable (such as the three just mentioned) is likely to be considered frivolous by the seller and a reason not to sell to you. Thus, the more escape clauses you include, the less likely you are to get the seller to sign. And the fewer escape clauses you include, the greater your risk in case you can't close the deal.

There may be, however, a way to help limit your liability in case you can't make the deal. Most modern purchase agreements include a *liquidated-damages clause.* If you sign this (and the seller does too), then the total amount of damages that you are likely to have to pay in the event you don't (or can't) make the deal is usually limited to your deposit. If you put up only $1,000 for a deposit, you don't have a great deal at risk.

However, it's a mistake to rely entirely on the liquidated-damages clause. A disgruntled seller can hire an attorney to challenge it, and you could spend a lot more money defending yourself in court.

Keep in mind that assigned purchase agreements tend to be rather iffy. There's a lot that can go astray in the time between signing them and actually concluding a sale between the seller and the rebuyer. If the sale can't be concluded, the seller is, of course, likely to get angry. And you want some good cover when that happens.

Are There Any Big Problems with Assignments?

There's an inherent problem in using an assignment to flip a property. It's simply that when most sellers discover that you're reselling the property at a substantial profit, they're likely to be unhappy. After all, they could conclude, what are you adding to the deal? They feel that your profit should rightly go into their pocket.

Never mind the fact that for whatever reason, they couldn't get the price you're reselling for on their own. (If they could've, they would've.) What you're bringing to the transaction is your marketing expertise.

As a result, you could have an angry seller on your hands who may refuse to sign off on the deal unless he or she gets more money or, even worse, wants to take you to court. To avoid just this sort of confrontation, it's important to inform the seller of what's going on.

TIP

Giving full disclosure to the seller (and the buyer) is the key to avoiding problems when using assignments.

Remember, even though it shouldn't make any difference what you do with property after you and the seller agree on a price, it's better to let the seller know up front what's happening to avoid any problems later on.

Should I Disclose to the Buyer Too?

Absolutely, yes. If you handle it wisely by letting the buyer know what you're paying for the property (and getting confirmation that he or she knows on a signed statement), there shouldn't be many problems. Indeed, the buyer may be impressed with your real estate acumen and want to work with you on a future deal!

On the other hand, if you conceal this information, that you're tying up the property for a low price and reselling at a higher, the buyer may discover it later on and think you were trying to pull a fast one, and go after you.

Keep in mind that most rebuyers won't care that you're flipping or how much you're making on the deal just as long as they're assured they aren't paying more than market price. If they see that they're getting a good deal, they will usually be satisfied.

Remember, the right way to handle a flip is to be sure that all parties know what you're doing (and get it in writing in case someone should later have an attack of memory failure).

What If I Can't Cash Out?

Sometimes it's hard to find a rebuyer who can come up with sufficient credit to get a mortgage at almost 100 percent or who can come up with sufficient cash to make a big down payment for a smaller mortgage. Therefore, you may find that to make a deal, it's to your advantage to get a second mortgage on a flip.

This works in the same ways as described above for options and assignments. However, in this scenario, when it's time for you to get your money out of the deal, there isn't enough cash to make it happen. So you give the rebuyer a second mortgage. You then get paid so much a month until you get all your money back, which usually happens a few years down the road when the rebuyer sells the property once again. (Alternatively, you could sell your second mortgage at a discount for cash. In the early years of the mortgage, however, expect the discount to be very heavy, as much as 50 percent, because the buyer of the mortgage assumes the risk that the rebuyer of the property won't keep making the payments.)

Of course, it goes without saying that you would want your rebuyer to be a good credit risk because if he or she defaults on the loan, you won't get all of your money out of the second mortgage. Many investors "age" these second mortgages for six months to a year before selling them for cash. Aged mortgages have a much smaller discount.

What Should I Know About Price Manipulation?

The source of the increasingly common perception that flipping is a shady practice is that over the past few years, unscrupulous investors have, in the process of flipping properties, manipulated mortgages, appraisals, and, most importantly, prices. Rather than do the real work of the transaction—namely, finding properties that are selling below market—they purchased properties at their actual market price and then, through manipulation, sold them for above market price to unwary buyers. This was done, apparently, in cooperation with lenders who secured higher appraisals than were warranted and made bigger loans than were justified. Often these properties were sold to poor minority rebuyers who really didn't understand market values or how high their payments should be. Subsequently, when these rebuyers couldn't make the stiff payments, they lost their houses to foreclosure.

That's where the real trouble started for these unscrupulous flippers. Almost all home mortgages are one way or another insured or guaranteed through the government or a government-related agency (FHA, VA, Fannie Mae, Freddie Mac, and so forth). When the government began taking these properties back, it found out what was happening and launched criminal investigations into the flippers.

This is not something you ever want to have happen to you. Always do the right thing: Start by finding undervalued properties—there are plenty of them out there to go around. Then, let everyone know what's happening in the deal, and get legitimate loans and appraisals. You'll do the seller, the rebuyer, the government, and even yourself a big favor.

Should I Always Flip a Property?

Sometimes you'll have the option. Either you can flip the property or you can hold it. What should you do? The answer is that whenever you can flip a property, do it. Don't hang onto the property.

The reason is simple. For every flippable property you find, you'll find a dozen or more perfectly acceptable properties that you can hold. Finding holders is easy; finding flippers is hard.

Further, you need the cash that flipping can generate. Holding properties tends to drain cash away. Often there is some small negative cash flow. And it can take years before you can get cash out of the holders in order to buy more properties.

There's really no big decision here. If you can generate cash from a flippable property, go for it. You can always find a holder tomorrow.

When Should I Check with
My Attorney?

Flipping properties is a great way to make quick money in real estate. But it's loaded with pitfalls. Therefore, be sure to check with a good real estate attorney before trying any flip.

As I said, that will cost you a few bucks, but it can also save you a lot of money and headaches in the long run.

11
Earning Profits from Rentals

If you're going to invest in real estate, at some point you will have rental properties and you will be a landlord. It will be up to you to find tenants, collect rents, clean up when tenants move out, and maintain and repair the properties. How well you do this will determine, to a large extent, how well you succeed in real estate.

In this chapter we'll go into the basics of what you need to know to be successful at rentals. We'll see what makes a good rental and how to keep it profitable:

- How to find a good rental property
- How to find good tenants
- How to keep good tenants
- How to profit from rentals

Keep in mind, however, that once you own rental property, you will need some very specific advice. For that you'll want to check into one of the many books written just on being a landlord. (I suggest my own: *The Landlord's Troubleshooter*, second edition, Dearborn, 1999.)

How Do I Find a Good Rental Property?

As noted in the first chapter, there are a lot of clues that you can look for to help you determine whether a home will make a good rental. If the property has these attributes (discussed at length in Chapter 1 and recapped here in brief), then chances are it will. If it doesn't, you'd be better off looking elsewhere:

Look in Areas with a Plentiful Supply of Tenants

In other words, you should look in areas where there are jobs near-by to supply a tenant base. Also, the type of worker should be suit-able to the rental. For example, if you have a low-income property and most of the local work force consists of highly paid white-collar workers, you might not find tenants easily. Similarly, if you have blue-collar workers in the area, you might have trouble find-ing tenants for a high-priced property. The property should match the tenant base.

Look in Areas with a Shortage of Rentals

Ideally yours will be the only rental in the area. Obviously, that's not going to happen. But if there are too many rentals chasing too few tenants, you'll have trouble. Check local newspapers for for-rent ads to get a sense of the supply. Also, visit a few of these rentals to learn what your competition is. And ask a few real estate agents who spe-cialize in rental properties what the rental market is like.

Look for Modern Homes

You don't want an older house that will require lots of repairs. Ideally, the home will be under 10 years old, preferably under 3. And it should be in good repair when you buy it (unless you're look-ing for a fixer-upper).

Don't Look for Elaborate Homes

Nothing fancy—you want beige carpeting, not white, which is easily soiled and difficult to clean. You want to avoid a swimming pool with high maintenance costs and lots of liability. A smaller lot with less landscaping to keep up is better. And so on.

Look for Homes That Offer Good Rental Incomes

Look for properties that offer a good ratio of rental income to cost. This is tricky. You want your monthly income from rents to come close to covering your expenses. The only way you can do this is to avoid overpaying for the property, which means that you'll want relatively "cheap" rentals. (See Chapter 4 for more information.)

Buy Close to Your Home

There's one last, but vitally important, criterion that we also discussed in the first chapter: Buy close to your own home.

TRAP

The single biggest mistake an investor can make is to buy rental property at a distance. It makes a nightmare out of renting up, collecting rents, and handling maintenance and repairs.

I made the mistake of buying at a distance when I first started in real estate and paid a price for it. Chances are, as you read this you'll be nodding to yourself and saying, Okay, that's his opinion. Let's move on. The problem, here, is that most people simply don't believe this is as serious a concern as it is, until they've experienced it. Then they can't believe how much trouble they're in.

If there's only one thing you get from this book, it should be, **don't buy rental properties far from home** (no more than half an hour away). That's how important I think this advice is.

How Do I Find Good Tenants?

Some investors complain that it's harder to find a good tenant than to find a good rental property! I don't believe that's the case. I've rented properties for more than three decades, and with only a few exceptions, I've always had good tenants. The simple rule here is that if you check out your tenants before you rent to them, you will avoid problems later on.

TIP

There are strict nondiscrimination laws with regard to renting. Get a complete set from HUD (800-767-7468) or an agent or local rental service. Basically they state that you can't discriminate in renting because of race, religion, sexual preference, occupation, educational status, medical status, or age of the tenant(s). You also can't refuse to rent to tenants with children if the home is big enough. You can, however, refuse to rent because of the financial condition of the tenants, provided that you apply your financial criteria across the board equally to everyone who applies.

How do you check out prospective tenants? You talk to them and get them to fill out a thorough rental application. (These are available in books that specialize in renting as well as from agents and attorneys.) The application includes permissions for you to run a credit check, contact current employers, and call previous landlords. When people apply to rent a house or apartment from you, there are five things to look for, as discussed below.

Obtain a Credit Report

Don't expect that all of your tenants will have sterling credit. Indeed, if they were wonderful credit risks, they likely would be owners instead of tenants. Rather, look for a history of making payments on time. If the applicant doesn't make timely payments on other bills, chances are the rent will be late too. You can get a credit report by contacting a local credit bureau. You can also have a local real estate agent run one for you. (Remember, you must have the applicant's permission to do this.)

Check with Previous Landlords

Make this call, and make sure it's not just to the current landlord (who may be willing to tell you anything to get rid of a bad tenant!). Most landlords will be unwilling to go into detail, but one question almost all will answer is, "Would you rent to this person again?" The answer can be very telling. (Remember, you should have permission to do this.)

Match the Tenant to the Property

If you have a big house, expect to rent to families with kids. If yours is a small place, be sure you don't get too many bodies in it. Also, keep track of the number of cars and motorcycles that tenants have. Too many will clog driveways and can become an eyesore.

Trust Your Instincts

When you talk with prospective tenants, how do you feel about them? Do they seem like people who will likely make the rent payments on time and keep the place up? Or do they seem like vagabonds who are interested only in quickly getting in and then paying slowly (or not at all) and messing up your place? I've found that heeding my gut feelings is often the best way to predict tenant behavior.

Verify Their Income

A tenant who doesn't have a job probably can't make the rent payments no matter how good the credit report seems. You'll want to call the current employer and verify the length of employment, likelihood of continued employment, and salary. (Be sure your application, signed by the prospective tenant, gives you permission to make this call.) Employers won't normally tell you an employee's salary but they will usually confirm a number that you give to them.

Offer a Clean Rental

In addition to the techniques mentioned above, you'll also want to be sure that you offer a good, clean rental. This means that the walls are freshly painted (or at least cleaned), the carpet is without stains and dirt, the appliances have been cleaned, and so forth. (It costs only about a hundred dollars to have a professional cleaning crew make a place spotless in just a few hours.)

The theory here is that if you have a dirty apartment, you won't find a clean tenant who will want to rent it. Rather, the only people who will rent a dirty apartment are tenants who won't keep things clean.

The way to find a clean tenant is to start out with a clean rental. It will appeal to the right kind of tenant for you.

How Much Should I Charge?

As noted in the first chapter, it's a good idea to charge a little below the prevailing market rates. For example, if rentals similar to yours are going for $1,000 a month, rent yours out for $950.

Obviously, you're going to rent faster because of the cheaper rent. But you'll also appeal to those tenants who are savvy about the market and know a good thing when they see it. In other words, a rental at slightly less than market often attracts a better tenant.

You can find out what similar properties are going for by becoming a pretend tenant for a weekend. Check out the rental properties in your area by going to see them. Talk to the owners. You can identify yourself as a landlord. Most other landlords will be happy to chat.

TIP

Check to see if there's a landlord's association in your area. Many have them. Consider joining or at least talking to some of the members to share information. This group can be particularly helpful in alerting you to bad tenants who may be in the area (those who move in, don't pay, mess up the property, and need to be evicted).

Should I Ask for the Money Up Front?

First-time landlords are sometimes hesitant about asking directly for their rent. Don't be. You're in the business of collecting rents, and you can't be shy about it. This is particularly the case when you're selecting a new tenant. I always ask for a substantial deposit. The deposit should go toward both the cleaning of the property after the tenant leaves as well as to maintain the security of the rental (in case there's damage or failure to pay rent).

There's much confusion about deposits. Technically, in most states the money you receive from a cleaning deposit is yours to spend when you receive it. However, when the tenant moves out, you're under an obligation to pay it back, provided that the tenant leaves the premises reasonably clean and without damage.

TIP

Some states require a landlord to keep deposits in a separate trust account and even to pay the tenants interest on the money. Check with a good agent who handles rentals in your area to find out if this applies to you.

The problem that many landlords get themselves into is that they spend the deposits as soon as they get them. Then they don't have the money on hand to pay back the tenants when they move out. Often, landlords in this situation try to rerent quickly and get a new deposit from a new tenant in order to repay the old. This is a kind of trap that's best to avoid. Even if not required by the state, I always keep tenants' deposits in a separate account, ready to return to them when required.

TIP

Most states require that landlords give a full accounting of deposits and pay back any unused portion within two to three weeks after the tenant moves out.

How Big Should the Tenants' Deposit Be?

The answer is, As big as possible. The more money the tenants put up as a deposit, the more responsible they are likely to be. They will always be eyeing that big deposit at the end of the tenancy, anticipating getting it back.

Many states, however, limit the maximum deposit amount, sometimes to one and a half or two times the monthly rental. In addition, there's also a limit to how much you can reasonably expect a tenant to come up with. For example, if your rent is $1,000 a month and you demand a $2,000 cleaning deposit, that's $3,000 to move in. You simply may not find that many tenants who have that much cash available. Thus, you may find that you're charging a smaller cleaning deposit in order to attract tenants.

Again, always ask for the deposit up front. Never allow the tenants to move in without paying *all* of it. A tenant who moves in having paid no deposit (or having made only a partial payment) will feel less pressured to look out for your premises. The deposit is your leverage, and you don't want to lose it.

Also, always get the first month's rent (or first and last if you're using a conventional lease) up front. Don't let the tenant move in with a partial payment.

The reason for getting the money up front may seem obvious, until you've been a landlord for a while and a future tenant pleads with you to accept partial payment. He or she may owe $2,500 to move in, but only have $1,250. Won't you please accept the $1,250 with the rest promised in only a week or two?

No, don't do it. A tenant who can't pay all the "move-in" money up front likely won't be able to make the monthly payments as they come due. This is an important rule not to overlook.

How Do I Keep Good Tenants?

You keep good tenants, once you have them, by making them happy. That may sound difficult, but it really isn't. Here are some easy to use guidelines that really do work:

Stay Out of Their Hair

Yes, come by once a month to collect the rent (unless they mail it in advance) and check out the property. But don't be there more often. They've rented the place and are entitled to "quiet enjoyment" of it. No tenant likes a snoopy landlord, and many will move out if you're too nosy. Leave your tenants alone, for the most part, and you'll do well. Of course, this applies only to the tenants who pay well and keep the place clean. It's a different story for bad tenants.

Always Take the Tenants' Calls

Usually tenants don't want to be your bosom buddy, so they will call only when there's a problem. But when there is a problem, they want someone else to be on the other of the line. You can maintain an answering service, an answering machine, or even a cell phone.

But, be sure that when the tenant calls, either you answer the phone or get back to him or her in a very timely fashion.

Fix Problems Fast

When the tenant calls, it could be a leaky faucet, a broken window, a stove that doesn't work, a dishwasher that spills water on the floor, or anything else. What you must do is quickly determine if it's the property's fault, or the tenant's fault. And usually you can't do this unless you zip out there to take a look. (Remember, you bought close to home, right?!) Once there, if it's the tenant's fault, explain that you'll have it fixed right away, but they'll have to pay for it. The money will come from their deposit, but then they'll have to pay to bring the deposit backup to its full level. If it's the property's fault (such as a broken hot water heater), tell them you'll fix it at your cost. And fix it immediately, within hours. While you might be willing to stay in a house without hot water (or whatever the problem is), tenants who are paying rent won't. They expect things to be fixed as soon as humanly possible. And unless you want to lose them, you'll see that it's, in fact, done just that fast.

Make Regular Upgrades to the House Fixtures and Features

Things wear out. Carpets get holes in them. Paint fades and gets dirty. None of these things are the fault of the tenant. They're just wear and tear caused by normal living. And you should plan on upgrading your rental over time. Some landlords do this every five years, some every three, some every seven. The whole idea is that if the tenant moves out because the place is run down due to your lack of maintenance, it's going to cost you more money (in advertising, lost rents, your time, and so on) than if you had fixed it to begin with. And for a new tenant, you'll need to spruce up the place anyway. Therefore, spend the money and keep the existing good tenant.

Avoid Being an Arrogant Landlord

What many unsuccessful landlords do is become arrogant. They feel that because they are the property *owner*, the lowly tenant should bow before them. Sort of like saying the tenant should be grateful to the landlord for providing a roof over his or her head.

That kind of thinking may have prevailed during the Middle Ages, but it has no place in modern day life. Rather, the landlord–tenant relationship is one of mutual benefits. You provide the housing—the tenant provides the rents. Neither is superior in some strange way to the other. If you don't like the tenant, you can ask him or her to move. You can also raise rents.

If the tenants don't like you or the rents you charge, they can move elsewhere. In short, tenants and landlords need each other.

If you can remember that it's strictly a business arrangement, you'll do better as a landlord.

How Do I Profit from Rentals?

As we've seen, profits from real estate usually come from selling for more than you paid. Inflation and shortages in the supply of housing (and other types of real estate) force prices up, and that allows you to make your profit.

However, there's another way to make money in real estate that we've only touched upon, and that's by collecting rents. When your rents are higher than your total expenses, you have positive cash flow. As that increases and you put more and more money in your pocket, you begin to make money from your rentals.

Generally speaking, when you buy a property, you lock in your expenses. (An exception would be if you have an adjustable-rate mortgage with which the interest rate and the monthly payment can fluctuate.) You do not, however, lock in your rental income. Over time, it should go up at least to match inflation and, if there's a shortage of rental property in the area, to beat inflation. The way you take advantage of this is to raise rents.

When Do I Raise Rents?

You raise rents when you can justify it given the rental market. Note, I didn't say you raise rents when you need more money, or when your have unexpected repairs, or when you think the tenant deserves to pay more. All these are irrelevant to your rental rate. The rate of rent you can charge depends entirely on what other landlords are charging for rents in your area. When rates go up overall, you can raise yours too.

Rental rates usually go up when a tenant moves out and the landlord rents the unit to the next tenant for more. This has a ripple effect across the market.

However, you can sometimes raise your rents for an existing tenant to slightly above the market rate.

Remember, we said that it makes sense to rent for slightly below market in order to quickly rent up to a good tenant. Once that tenant is in your unit for a year or so, however, some degree of inertia begins to take effect. It becomes hard for the tenant to move out. There's the hassle of finding a new apartment, of dealing with the movers, of changing the utilities, mail, and phone, and on and on. In other words, all things being equal, tenants who are basically happy with where they live would rather not move if they could choose not to do so.

Of course, if you raise their rent, they'll reconsider. They'll immediately go out and see what else is available. They'll comparison price shop.

If other similar units are renting for more, they certainly will stay with you.

If other similar units are renting for about the same, they'll certainly stay with you.

However, if other similar units are renting for just a little bit less, chances are they will still stay with you simply to avoid the hassle of moving.

Thus, if you raise the rent from $950 to $1,000 when similar units are renting for $975, most tenants will pay the extra amount. It's simply easier than moving.

TIP

Avoid big rent increases because they unnerve tenants and make them more likely to jump ship. Also, try to do something for the tenant, such as repainting or recarpeting, before you raise the rent.

As you can see, if you're very careful, once you have the tenant settled in, you can sometimes raise the rent and charge an above-market rental rate. Push it too far, however, and you'll lose the tenant.

How Do I Get Rid of Bad Tenants?

Bad tenants usually fall into two categories: Either they pay late (or don't pay at all!), or they make a mess of the property. Chronic behavior of one or both types suggests that you may be better off without the tenant. (Sometimes you simply want to get rid of a tenant to put yourself in a better state of mental health!)

If you have a month-to-month tenancy, normally a 30-day notice to move is all it takes. With a lease, however, the tenant has the right to keep the property (as long as the conditions of the lease are met) until the term is up, often a year or more. To get rid of a bad tenant in a lease, you may actually have to pay them off! This could mean giving them several months' rent to move out. (You'd only do this for a tenant you really couldn't stand!)

Of course, the ultimate way to remove a tenant who won't pay is eviction. This involves an unlawful-detainer court action. You'll need an attorney at least the first time you try it.

If you "mind the store" and raise rents when appropriate, keep good tenants and get rid of bad ones, over time you'll find that your rewards in the form of positive cash flow from your rental property will positively amaze you!

12

Identifying Tax Advantages in Real Estate Investments

If you make a profit, you'll probably have tax to pay on it. It's just that simple. However, you may not have to pay that tax right away, or ever, depending on how you apply the tax code. In this chapter we'll take a look at real estate taxation.

SPECIAL NOTE

What follows is not tax advice. It is simply an overview of some of the federal tax rules affecting real estate investment property. For tax advice, you need to consult with a tax professional such as an accountant or tax attorney.

Calculating Depreciation

If you own investment real estate, you can depreciate it. When you *depreciate* real estate, you consider a certain percentage of its "cost" (we'll talk more about cost later) each year as a reduction in the value of the property.

Almost all business assets can be depreciated. Cars, for example, are depreciated over a life span of five years. In a straight-line method, you might take 20 percent a year of the cost of the car each year over five years as a loss of value. Residential real estate must be depreciated over 27.5 years. Again using a straight-line method (equal parts taken each year), you would take 1/27.5 of the value (usually the purchase price plus transaction costs less the value of the land) each year as a loss.

Of course, the value of property goes up, not down. So how can you take a loss on an asset that's increasing in value? A helpful way to understand this is to think of it as a "paper loss." Most assets deteriorate over time. Even a house will eventually fall away to dust. So instead of simply waiting until the end of its useful life span (arbitrarily decided by the government), you take a portion of the loss in value each year.

TIP

The time span of 27.5 years is specified by the government, and it is quite arbitrary. In the past much shorter time spans have been allowed.

But, you may reasonably wonder, while the house will eventually deteriorate, the land never will. How do you depreciate land costs? The answer is, you can't. You can depreciate only the building, not the land. The only exception would be land that had an asset that was depletable, such as gas or oil, and that's not the case here.

Is Depreciation an Expense?

Yes, it is. As you can see in the following list, it's an expense like your other rental property expenses.

Typical Rental Property Expenses

- Mortgage interest
- Taxes
- Insurance
- Water service
- Garbage service
- Maintenance and repair
- Fix-up

- Advertising
- Pool and garden services
- Depreciation

TIP

Save all your receipts! In contrast to tax accounting for the home you live in for which the only deductions are typically property taxes and mortgage interest, for a rental property you own, almost everything is deductible. You may even be able to deduct a phone, auto, even business cards and other expenses you incur in managing the property! Check with your accountant.

If you keep track of your rental property expenses on a monthly basis, it is a simple matter of adding them up at the end of the year to figure out your tax situation.

To do that, you subtract your total annual expenses from your total annual income, and the result is your profit or loss.

Does Depreciation Contribute to Loss?

It certainly does. As soon as you begin to look at properties out there in the real world, you'll come to realize that there are few properties for which the income comes even close to paying for the actual cash expenses. When you add the paper loss of depreciation to your cash expenses, you almost always find that there's a loss for the year:

Typical Yearly Income and Expenses on a Rental House

Total annual income	$14,440	($1,200 monthly)
Total annual cash expenses	14,000	
Positive cash flow	440	
Annual depreciation	7,500	
Annual loss	−7,060	

Once depreciation is subtracted, there is almost always a loss as a result, at least on paper. In the example above, an income-generating property that actually shows a positive cash flow (more money coming in than cash expenses going out) turns into a big loser as soon as depreciation is subtracted from the income.

TIP

Remember that the loss from depreciation is not an out-of-pocket expense. It's simply an accounting loss— it shows up only on paper.

In the dim past, depreciation was a tax dodge that was used by the wealthy to reduce their sizeable incomes. They would take the loss from the depreciation of their real estate (that occurred only on paper) and deduct it from their ordinary income. That reduced their ordinary income, which, of course, reduced the amount of taxes they would owe on that income.

That tax shelter was eliminated for the wealthy by the Tax Reform Act of 1986. Now it is available only if your income is less than $150,000. We'll have more to say about this shortly.

How Does Depreciation Reduce the Tax Basis of the Property?

Earlier we said that depreciation reduces the "cost" of the building by a certain amount each year. The cost we were referring to is the price the owner paid to buy the building, and that price is used as a starting point for computing the tax basis. Other costs that are considered part of the tax basis are such expenses as closing costs. Once the tax basis is established for the property, it is used to determine the owner's profit or loss on the property over time. If the owner sells the property, the selling price is compared to the tax basis to determine whether the owner had a capital gain or loss.

The tax basis, as we said, for most assets including real estate property is their cost. However, with real estate, other considerations can affect the basis. For example, you have to pay substantial transaction fees when you buy property. Most of these fees are added to the basis. If you were to build an addition to the home, the cost of the addition would also be added to the basis.

On the other hand, the basis may be reduced. For example, depreciation reduces the basis of the property. Here's how it works:

Change in Tax Basis due to Depreciation

Original basis (cost)	$200,000
Room added on	+ 30,000
Adjusted basis	230,000
Depreciation ($7,000 annually for 10 years)	−70,000
New adjusted basis	160,000

Notice that although the property began with a basis of $200,000, which was its cost, that basis went up when a room was added, and more importantly here, it went down when depreciation was calculated.

Calculating Capital Gains

What Is the Importance of the Tax Basis?

Understanding the tax basis is important because it (and the sales price) determines the capital gains tax you'll have to pay when you sell. Your capital gain on the property is the difference between the adjusted tax basis and the sales price.

Calculating Capital Gain

Sales price (adjusted for costs of sale such as commission)	$300,000
Adjusted tax basis	160,000
Capital gain (on which tax is due)	140,000

Thus, returning to our example, you buy the property for $200,000, add a room for $30,000, which raises your basis, and then depreciate the property for $70,000, which lowers the basis. When you sell, both the raising and lowering of the tax basis affect the amount of your capital gain.

TIP

It's important to keep one's eye on the donut and not on the hole. In general, the higher the tax basis, the lower the capital gain. Therefore, although deducting a depreciation expense may make sense in the immediate term, doing so will lower the tax basis in the long term when the property is sold and increase the amount subject to the capital gains tax, which will result in higher taxes.

All of which is to say that while depreciating real estate can produce a tax write-off, as noted earlier, when you sell, that tax loss comes back to haunt you as a capital gain.

How Were Capital Gains Treated in the Past?

In decades past, anyone, regardless of his or her income, could write off losses on real estate. What they were actually doing, however, was converting their ordinary income to capital gain income because income from capital gains was taxed at a lower rate than ordinary income.

The preceding explanation went by rather fast, so let's take it again a bit slower. Let's consider just one year. In that year the property sustained a loss of $7,000 (primarily from depreciation). That $7,000 was then deducted from the investor's ordinary income. That meant that the investor avoided paying ordinary income taxes (read "at a high tax rate") on $7,000.

Then the very next year, that property sold, and it showed a $7,000 capital gain attributable to depreciation. The investor then had to pay tax on this amount. However, because it was a "capital gain" as opposed to "ordinary income," the tax rate was lower. Thus the great tax shelter benefit in real estate was that it converted ordinary income to capital gains, which were taxed at a lower rate.

How Are Capital Gains Treated Now?

So, can I convert my ordinary income to capital gains and reduce my tax rate? Not really, for two reasons. First, the Tax Reform Act of 1986 forbade high-income investors from taking a deduction on their real estate losses. Then the Taxpayer Relief Act of 1997 reduced the capital gains rate (and added a few more wrinkles, as we'll shortly see).

To begin, however, let's consider the rules with regard to taking a loss from real estate as a deduction against your ordinary income. What is considered ordinary income under the existing rules?

Active income. The tax law now discriminates among the types of income that we receive. Income from wages or as compensation for services is called *active income.* It includes commissions, consulting fees, salary, or anything similar. It's important for those involved in real estate to note that profits and losses from businesses in which you "materially participate" (not included are limited partnerships) are included. However, activities from real estate are specifically excluded.

Passive income. This is a bit trickier to define, but in general *passive income* means the profit or loss that we receive from a business activity in which we do *not* materially participate. This includes not only limited partnerships but also income from any real estate that is rented out. It's important to note that real estate is specifically defined as "passive."

Portfolio income. Income from dividends, interest, royalties, and anything similar is considered *portfolio income.* We need not worry much about this here except to note that it does not include real estate income.

Under the old law, income was income and loss was loss. You could thus deduct any loss on real estate from your other income. Under the current law your personal income is considered "active" while your real estate loss is considered "passive." Since you can't deduct a passive loss from an active income, you can't, in general, write off any real estate losses.

How Does the "Little Guy" Handle Capital Gains?

We've already said that this tax reform was aimed primarily at the wealthy to eliminate a big tax shelter. But there is an advantage in the tax reform law for the small investor. This advantage is in an important exception to the above rules. The exception provides a $25,000 allowance for write-offs for taxpayers whose ordinary income is in a lower tax bracket. In other words, you can write off up to $25,000 in losses from real estate against your active income provided that your income is below the specified ceiling and that you meet certain other qualifications:

1. *Your gross adjusted income must not exceed $150,000.* If your income is below $100,000, then you qualify for the entire $25,000 exception. If it is between $100,000 and $150,000, you lose 50 cents of the allowance for every dollar your income exceeds $100,000.

   Since most small investors have an ordinary income under $150,000, the allowance applies to them. They can deduct some of their losses on real estate up to the $25,000 limitation.

2. *You must actively participate in the business of renting the property.* This can be tricky—after all, what does "actively participate" really mean?

   Obviously, if you own the property and are the only person directly involved in handling the rental—you advertise it, rent it, handle maintenance and clean-up, collect the rent, and so on—then you materially participate.

   However, there are gray zones. Generally if you don't personally determine the rental terms, approve new tenants, sign for repairs, approve capital improvements, and the like, then you may not qualify.

   The question always comes up, "What if I hire a management firm to handle the property for me?"

   Using a management firm is even grayer. In general, employing a management firm is probably okay as long as you continue to materially participate (determine rental terms, approve new tenants, sign for repairs, approve capital improvements, and the like). If you are going to use a management firm, be sure that you have your attorney check over the agreement you sign with the firm to see that it does not characterize you as not materially participating and thus prevent you from deducting any loss.

Are There Any Other Kinks in the Rules?

On the surface, the allowance and the qualifications may seem straightforward. But, they can be tricky. For example, here are some other considerations:

1. The income used to determine whether you qualify is your gross adjusted income. This means your income after you have taken some deductions such as retirement plan contributions (not IRAs), alimony, or moving expenses.

2. The allowance does not apply to farms. If you materially participate in the running of a farm, other rules apply. See your accountant or tax attorney.

3. Those who don't qualify for taking the deduction against their active income cannot likewise take the deduction against their portfolio income. (Remember that portfolio income comes from interest, dividends, royalties, and so on.)

So When I Sell, I Will Probably Owe Some Capital Gains Taxes?

Yes, assuming you don't sell for a loss. However, as noted, the capital gains tax rate has been reduced. At the present time it's a maximum of 20 percent. Hence, even if you do have to pay, it won't be a confiscatory amount.

TRAP

You owe tax on a capital gain regardless of whether the property is an investment or your personal residence. However, if you sell at a capital loss, while you can take that loss on investment property, you can't take a deduction against that loss if it's on a personal residence! A quirk in the tax laws.

Is There Any Legal Way to Avoid a Tax on My Profits?

That, of course, is the national pastime that most Americans play—how to legally avoid paying high taxes. And, in the case of investment real estate, there are a few loopholes that can benefit the investor.

The first method that might be used is to convert the property from an investment to a personal residence. You can remove the tenants and move in yourself, declaring the property your principal residence. After a period of time, you may then be able to sell the home and reap the benefits of the principal-residence capital gains exclusion of up to $500,000.

TIP

Keep in mind that in real estate you owe taxes only on your profit (capital gain) when you sell. No matter how high the value of your property goes, you don't pay income tax on that increase as long as you continue to own it. (You would, of course, owe income taxes if you showed excess income over expenses on an annual basis.)

There are certain problems with the above scenario, however. The first is, how long must you reside in the property to make it your personal residence? I don't know of any hard-and-fast rule. Some accountants say two years, others longer. Check with your professional tax advisor.

The second has to do with all that depreciation you took while you owned the property. Under the current law, it is recaptured at a special rate. Thus, even though you may avoid paying taxes on most of your capital gain by using the personal-property exclusion (noted below), you might still owe some taxes on the recaptured depreciation losses that you earlier took.

TIP

Yet another problem here is that very often the investor is not really interested in moving into the rental property. In that case, a tax-deferred exchange, as described below, might be better.

The Exclusion-up-to-$500,000 Rule Under the 1997 Taxpayer Relief Act, each person regardless of age can exclude up to $250,000 of the capital gain on a principal residence. For a couple, that multiplies up to $500,000.

TIP

The exclusion can be taken only on a principal residence. It *cannot* be taken on investment property unless that investment property was previously converted to a principal residence.

There are some fine-print rules involved in the exclusion that your professional tax advisor can explain to you, but the big rule to keep in mind is that in order to obtain the exclusion, you must have lived in the property for 2 of the previous 5 years. That means two things: First, you've got to live in the property (not just own it) for two years before you can claim the exclusion. Second, you can claim the exclusion only once every two years. Thus, if you own 15 rental properties, it would take you 30 years at minimum to bail out of all of them in this fashion!

The Section 1031(a)(3) Tax-Deferred Exchange *Is there another way I can legally avoid paying taxes on my capital gain?* Yes, there is. You can trade your property for another and defer the capital gain from the old property to the new. This is technically called a *Section 1031(a)(3) Tax Deferred Exchange.*

A great many investors see this as a means of multiplying their profits without paying taxes along the way. They hopscotch from property to property, increasing the value of their real estate holdings unencumbered by paying taxes for each transaction.

TIP

It's sort of like getting compound interest on your equity. Normally, in a strict sale and then purchase of another property, you would pay taxes on your capital gain. That would leave you less equity to invest in the next property. However, by deferring that tax bill into the future, you have all your equity to put into the next property, meaning you can buy a bigger and better investment house!

The rules governing tax-free exchanges were greatly simplified over a decade ago by several tax cases, and the most famous was the Starker case, which ultimately resulted in the *Starker rule.* Under Starker, you just go ahead and sell your investment property as you would otherwise. However, you have 45 days before or after the sale to designate a new property into which you will invest your money. And you have 120 days to close the deal on that new property.

Note that there are other strict conditions on the exchange that must be met. One is that you may not take a cash-out ("boot") as part of the sale. If you want cash out, you must usually refinance the old property before the exchange or the new property after it. Again, check with your accountant for details.

Another condition is that only like-kind properties can be exchanged. In our case that usually means property held for investment purposes—for example, a rental house for a rental duplex, a lot for a lot. Exchanging an apartment building for an oil well might not be allowed by the IRS.

Combining an Exchange and a Personal-Property Exclusion One of the problems we noted earlier with converting an investment property into a personal property was that you may not want to reside in a property you own as an investment. If that's the case, then the answer could be simple. Just make a tax-deferred exchange of the investment property for a property in which you would like to live. Then convert the desirable home from an investment to principal residence.

Keep in mind, however, the "like-kind" rule noted above. A personal residence is not the same as an investment house. Therefore, in order to not invalidate the tax-deferred status of the exchange, you might have to rent out the new property for a time before moving in yourself. How long must the property be rented out before it is converted to a principal residence? Some tax advisors have suggested six months, others as long as two years. Again, check with your own professional tax advisor.

Keeping Good Records

From our discussion in this chapter, one other thing should be apparent: You need to have good records. It's very important that you keep every receipt and note every expense and piece of income in a ledger.

At some time you may have to prove to the IRS that the expenses you have reported on your investment property were real. For example, three years earlier you had a vacancy, and you spent $115 on advertising to get a new tenant. Prove it, says the IRS. So, you reach into your bag of receipts and pull out an invoice from the local paper for $115 for advertising. Attached to it is a copy of the ad itself and your check in payment. There's no disputing that.

Also, keep all records of any improvements you make to the property. Remember, improvements *raise* the tax basis, which will later reduce the amount of capital gains taxes you will need to pay. (The higher the tax basis, the lower the capital gain and consequently the lower the capital gain taxes.) If you make a capital improvement, such as put on a new roof or add a patio, keep those receipts too. At the end of the year your accountant will be able to use them to adjust your tax basis upward.

TIP

Just because you spend money improving your rental, don't assume that you've made a capital improvement for tax purposes. Replacing a water heater, for example, may not be a capital improvement. It may be considered a repair. Adding a tile roof where there was previously a less expensive tar roof would be a capital improvement (at least the difference in price between the tar roof and the tile roof).

Refinancing

As strange as it may seem, refinancing your property without a sale has no immediate tax consequences. You don't report new mortgages to the IRS. If you get cash out, you will, however, have less equity to rely upon later when you do sell and must pay capital gains taxes.

Avoiding the IRS Label
"Dealer in Real Estate"

In this chapter we've assumed that you would have capital gains tax
to deal with when you sell your property. However, if you buy and
sell many properties, particularly within a single year, the IRS may
qualify you as a "dealer in real estate." What that means is that your
profits are then all considered to be personal income, not capital
gains, and the tax can be significantly higher. Check with your
accountant.

If I've conveyed nothing else to you in this chapter, I hope that I
have given you the impression that buying and selling real estate
goes hand in hand with tax considerations. If you're a wise investor,
you'll consult with your tax professional each time before you make
a new move.

Portions of this chapter first appeared in Buy, Rent & Sell, *Robert Irwin,
McGraw-Hill, 2000.*

13
Financing for Investors

In the old days (read about 10 years ago), getting investor financing was almost impossible. Just mention that you were buying the property for investment purposes (or even worse that you were an investor who wanted to take cash out) and lenders would run, not walk, in the other direction. An investor was a pariah to the lending industry.

That has largely (but not entirely) changed. Financial profiling has revolutionized the lending industry. Now lenders can take a snapshot of your finances (income, assets, expenses, properties, and so on) and almost instantaneously determine whether or not you'll qualify for a mortgage. And loans are available.

Generally speaking, they're not as good for investors as for people who are buying property to live in. But they're not bad. In short, today investor financing is much easier to obtain than ever before.

How Do I Get the Best Mortgage When I Buy?

As noted in the first chapter, the way to get the best deal on a mortgage is to not be an investor but instead to be an owner-occupant. For owner-occupants with a good credit history and adequate income, loans are available with a *loan-to-value* (LTV) *ratio* as high as 103 percent (for "conforming" loans to $307,000). If you are prepared to live in the property, the very best financing in the world is available to you.

It's important to understand, however, that we're not talking here about pretending to be an owner-occupant. We're talking about actually moving into the home and living there—occupying it.

The great temptation for investors is to say they will live in the property in order to get the good financing and then not actually move in. By so doing, they take advantage of better financing than they could get as an investor. The reason for not moving in, of course, is that they may already have a house in which they live and they don't want to lose even a month's worth of rent from the property they are buying.

No matter what you call this, it's simple lying, and if you do it, it could land you in real hot water. Lenders are on the alert for people who say they are moving in when in reality they intend to rent out the property. To confirm that you've moved in, a lender may call after a month or two to check. Or they may send your payment books to your attention at the new home's address with "no forwarding" requested. Or they may even send someone by three months later to see how you're doing. If a tenant answers the door, the ruse is up.

Almost all mortgages are in some way insured, guaranteed, or resold through government or quasi-government agencies. That means that if you lie and are caught, you will have to do a lot of explaining to the Treasury Department. Penalties could be anything from a demand to immediately repay the full amount of the loan to indictment on criminal charges.

All of which is to say if you're going to put down that you intend to occupy the property, be sure you in fact do that. Later on, after you've lived there for a while, you can think about converting it to a rental.

Are Investor Mortgages Available?

They certainly are. Although the LTV, the borrower's qualifications, and the interest rates change from time to time, generally speaking these loans require a bigger down payment and a higher personal income, and they are sometimes written at a slightly higher rate of interest and more points.

Recently investor mortgages have become available with an LTV ratio of 90 percent. Some are written at about an eighth to a half percent higher interest rate than owner-occupant loans, and they include about an extra point to pay (assuming, of course, that the investor is buying a single-family home or condo). Some lenders, however, claim that they will fund investor mortgages with no interest/points premiums.

Additionally, there's a little trick that lenders use for investors who already have rental property that results in the investors' needing a higher personal income to qualify. If you own rental property, the lenders will not allow you apply all of the rental income you receive toward the new financing. On the other hand, they will require you to note all of the expenses you have. (Recently they were allowing only about 75 percent of the income.) That means that even if your property breaks even, you still need some extra income in order to balance out the expenses. That's why an investor with multiple properties needs a higher income to qualify for the same mortgage as an owner-occupant would receive.

You obtain an investor mortgage from the same place you get an owner-occupant loan—a mortgage broker or bank. You simply state what you want the loan for, and the broker or bank will do all the paperwork.

In addition, there's also an option of financing the property through the seller, which we'll discuss shortly.

How Do I Get Cash Out?

In the past this was the single most difficult problem for investor. You might have owned a solid rental property that was producing a positive cash flow. Yet, when you wanted to cash out some of your equity, lenders would simply turn their backs on you.

Today, it's a somewhat different story. In many cases you can get an 80 percent mortgage including cash back to you. In some cases, 90 percent is available with cash back on a refinancing. But you do have to search around. Again, you'll pay a stiffer interest rate and more points, and you will need more personal income to qualify. But at least the financing is there.

An alternative to the preceding scenario involves obtaining a second mortgage. Many banks offer these loans to investors. Generally speaking, the *combined loan-to-value* (CLTV) *ratio* is the same as it would be for a large first mortgage—80 to 90 percent. However, the higher interest rate and points apply only to the second mortgage. When this type of second mortgage is paired with a lower-interest-rate first mortgage, the combined interest rate sometimes can be lower than it would be for a single large new refinanced mortgage. It's something to consider.

TIP

I have seen some lenders include in their documentation a prohibition against later renting out property bought by a person as an owner-occupant. Check with your attorney, but I've never seen a case where this was enforced.

What about Seller Financing?

Some of the best financing for an investor actually comes from sellers. Sellers often don't care whether or not you intend to occupy the property or rent it out. Indeed, many simply don't ask. Further, sometimes sellers are eager to give the buyer financing. If you find a seller in this position, you can get some surprisingly good financing deals.

Why Would a Seller Want to Finance a Buyer?

One reason a seller would want to finance a buyer is that the seller is having trouble selling the property. He or she hopes that by offering the buyer financing, the sale will be quick. In this situation the seller often anticipates that the buyer will have some credit problems (else why wouldn't the buyer get institutional financing?) and is prepared to accept it. Thus, if you can't get an institutional loan for one reason or another, seller financing is probably your best alternative. (Interestingly, seller financing is often so good that many very successful investors buy property *only* when they can get seller financing.)

A second reason that sellers might want to finance a sale is that they are looking to invest their money in a bond of some type that will pay them a high interest rate, like a mortgage. This is particularly the case with older sellers who may have paid off, or nearly so, their original mortgage. If they get cash for the sale of their house, they might want to avoid the risk of other investment vehicles, preferring instead to simply stick their money in a bank or in a CD and collect the interest. However, a mortgage typically pays higher interest, so they are thrilled if you give them a mortgage instead. (Recently banks were paying under 2 percent interest, while home mortgages were paying close to 7 percent—a real incentive for a free-and-clear seller to opt to handle the financing.)

How Do I Arrange It?

Seller financing (also called *creative financing*) is arranged at the time you make your purchase offer. Instead of putting into the purchase offer a standard contingency that the sale is subject to your obtaining a new mortgage from an institutional lender, you say that the sale is subject to the seller's giving you financing. Of course, you include the desired interest rate, points (if any), term, and so forth. In other words, you make the deal contingent upon obtaining seller financing. If the seller won't give it to you, there's no deal. Make the price good enough, and any seller will at least seriously consider the offer.

TIP

Keep in mind that the seller must be able to offer you financing. That means the seller must own the home free and clear, or there must be a mortgage on it that you can assume with the seller's financing his or her equity (you're getting a new first loan and the seller is financing his or her equity in a second mortgage). If the seller has virtually no equity in the property (the mortgage is close to the value), then no seller financing is possible.

In today's market, most sellers are intent on getting cash out. Frequently they need the money to plunk down on the next house they are buying. However, occasionally you'll come across a seller who has other plans for the equity. In this instance, seller financing may be possible. Just keep in mind that, unlike cash offers, you may need to make many offers on many houses before you find a seller who is amenable.

How Do I Qualify for Seller Financing?

As noted earlier, the beauty of seller financing is that there is no formal qualifying. However, most sellers will want to be at least assured that you have the wherewithal to make the mortgage payments. (Any good real estate agent will insist that you demonstrate this.)

Therefore, a credit report is typically run, and sometimes income verification (where your employer confirms your employment longevity and salary) and deposit verification (where your bank confirms how much money you have on hand) are conducted. These checks can be handled by most agents.

It's then up to the seller to determine if you're sufficiently worthy to buy the property and to be given seller financing. However, unlike institutional lenders, usually there's no computer scoring or other arcane techniques for evaluating your creditworthiness. Rather, it's just a seller's guess. And the more anxious sellers are to get rid of the property, the more likely they are to accept less than sterling qualifying on your part.

Are Other Types of Financing Available?

The first rule in real estate is that everything is negotiable, and the second rule is that creativity pays. So, yes, there are all sorts of other types of financing available.

For example, I've seen family financing. A son or daughter may want to buy an investment house. They have the income to handle it, but not the cash. So the parents pop for the down payment and closing costs. Then they share ownership. Typically the son or daughter will handle the management of the property, and when it's time to sell, the family will split up the profits.

This system, of course, is not limited to families. It will work with friends or even perfect strangers. However, a word of caution: Put everything in writing. People, even friends, even close relatives, often forget what was said months or years earlier. When it's time to sell, you want to have in writing exactly how the profits (or if something goes wrong, the losses) are to be split up. Further, you want to be sure that there are solid escape clauses allowing you, or another party, to exit the deal if situations change. (For example, you could lose your job, or your sibling, friend, or son or daughter could need to move out of the area.)

All of which is to say that if you intend to use any type of shared financing, spend the bucks to have a good attorney draw up a rock-solid agreement. It won't cost that much, and it could save lots of hassle and money later on.

TIP

 The tax advantages of property ownership (deduction of taxes, interest, and other expenses on investment property) can be divided in many different ways among shared owners. If you are interested in doing this, before you draw up any agreements, find out from your accountant or tax attorney exactly how to handle the tax formulas and required paperwork.

Asset-Based Financing

Yet another type of financing is to borrow not on the property you are buying but on other property such as stocks or bonds that you already own. The advantage in securing this type of financing is that you can obtain loans at very low interest rates, often through stock-brokers and banks.

Another financing method that experienced real estate investors frequently use is to borrow on property they already own in order to make a new purchase. For example, you may have three rental homes in which you have substantial equity. You can refinance these properties (either with individual loans or with a blanket loan on all three) and use the funds to buy a fourth house. If you've ever played the game *Monopoly®*, you already know the basics of how this method works.

Other Financing

As you can see, the types and sources of real estate financing available to you as an investor are limited only by your imagination. Don't feel boxed in by rules you imagine exist. If you can come up with a creative idea, try it. It just might work.

For example, some people finance their real estate purchase (at least the down payment) with cash they borrow on their credit cards. Is this a good way for you to buy property? No, it's not because the interest rate on credit cards (often 20 percent or higher) will kill you in the long run. I've seen some people try this creative approach only to eventually lose their property to foreclosure. But I've also seen other people use their credit cards on a short-term basis, and succeed. So in the right circumstances, it can work. If you need to borrow the money for a month or two and then you replace it with a permanent long-term loan, sure, using your credit cards might very well work.

Be creative. But have a plan. And before you take action, talk it over with a financial advisor such as a good real estate agent, tax attorney, or accountant.

14

FAQs (and Answers)

The following are frequently asked real estate investment questions drawn from several sources including robertirwin.com. If you have questions you'd like answered or would like to learn about other books by Robert Irwin, check out this website.

Agents

Working with More Than One Agent

Should I work with only one agent, or should I "play the field" and have a lot of agents looking for property for me?

A good rule to remember in real estate is that loyalty offered is loyalty returned. If you're loyal to one agent (presumably a good one!), that agent will turn over every stone looking for just the right property for you. On the other hand, if you work with lots of different agents, none of them is likely to work hard for you out of concern that even if they find a good property for you, you'll buy through someone else.

Switching Agents

Can I switch agents if mine isn't working hard?

You can and should. If an agent doesn't call you at least once a week to let you know what he or she is doing for you, chances are he or she isn't doing much for you. As an investment buyer, it's very easy to simply switch to another agent.

Working with a Buyer's Agent

Should I work with a buyer's agent?

You should work with an agent who declares that he or she is a buyer's agent. That means he or she has a fiduciary obligation to represent you, not the seller. Any agent can make this kind of declaration.

Beware of dealing with a seller's agent. He or she may convey any weakness you express to the seller.

I've heard you and other real estate experts say that buyers should always use their own brokers when purchasing a property. I'd like to do that, but I don't want to pay the commission. Is there any way I can use a buyer's agent without paying the commission?

This is one instance in which you can have your cake and eat it too. In most cases, the sellers, not the buyers, end up paying the buyer's agent's commission. Here's how it works. You get a buyer's agent to work for you. Since almost 90 percent of properties are listed by agents who will cobroke (will split the commission with another agent), your buyer's agent should be able to work out a deal where he or she gets paid, in effect, by the seller. The seller's commission is split between buyer's agent and seller's agent.

Normally, it's only when the selling agent won't cobroke that you could be liable for the buyer's agent's commission. And in that situation, you can choose not to buy the home.

You should carefully check any agreement your buyer's agent wants you to sign to be sure that you're not committed to paying a commission if it can be obtained by cobroking and that you always have the option of not buying a home. (Show the agreement to your attorney if you're not sure.) Some buyer's agents do insist that buyers pay their fee no matter what. However, I certainly wouldn't sign such an agreement in today's market.

Negotiating Commissions

What's the "fair" commission rate I should pay an agent to sell my investment single-family home? If I sell it myself, as a FSBO, and an agent brings me a buyer, do I owe him or her a commission?

It's important to remember that in real estate there is no "set" or "fair" commission rate. Rather, everything is up for negotiation.

Further, if you sell your home "by owner"—that is, as a FSBO—normally you would not expect to pay a commission at all. However, if a buyer's broker brought you a purchaser with a signed contract ready to buy, you might agree to pay that agent half a commission, which is the usual split in most areas. For example, if the average commission in your area is 6 percent (it could just as easily be 5 or 7 percent) and a buyer's broker brings you a buyer ready, willing, and able to purchase, then that broker would reasonably expect to get 3 percent.

In today's market agents in many parts of the country are agreeing to do much of the paperwork involved in a transaction for anywhere from $500 to $1,500. If you're on the East Coast, a standard attorney's fee for handling your end of the transaction would be roughly that amount.

Working with Discount Brokers

When selling our investment property, we want to list with a broker. But some brokers are now advertising that they will sell for a reduced commission, sometimes as low as 1 percent. Does it pay to go with a reduced commission agent?

The question is usually one of service versus cost. You can't normally expect to get the same service from a discount broker as you can from a full-service agent (although some discount agents advertise full service). Typically for the discount, you are expected to do some of the work. That may include paying for advertising, showing the house yourself, negotiating with potential buyers, and managing the escrow. In most cases the agent will handle the documentation but not in all. It's important to remember that few things in life offer a free ride, and real estate is no exception. Someone has to do the work. If you pay full price, the agent will do the work for you. It you get a discount, you may have to do some of the work yourself.

The situation is somewhat different with regard to finding a buyer. It's important that your home be listed with the Multiple Listing Service (MLS) so that all other brokers in the area will have an opportunity to work on it. However, a buyer's broker's fee (as noted above) is typically 3 percent. I wouldn't list it on the MLS for any less and expect good service.

A discount broker may charge as little as 1 percent, but that's usually only for the selling agent's fee. It can be another 3 percent for the buyer's agent's fee (and the MLS listing—see above).

Ultimately, if your property presents well and is correctly priced, it should sell either with a full-service or a discount broker. The difference is in how much of the selling work you do and how long it takes to sell.

Finding a Good Agent

How do I evaluate a real estate agent? Most seem pretty much alike. What criteria should I use to differentiate them?

A good real estate agent is part financial advisor, part marriage counselor, and part confidant. And, of course, you expect them to know all about real estate. I would expect anyone who had all of those qualities to be at the least:

1. *Honest:* You want the agent to tell you when you're offering too little (or asking too much). You should be on the alert to sense if the agent is patronizing you just to get your business.

2. *Assertive:* You want the agent to be aggressive enough to get sellers (or buyers) to accept your price, yet not so demanding that he or she intimidates you into accepting a price other than what you want.

3. *Professional:* I would never list with an agent who runs down other agents or other people in the field.

4. *Experienced:* Whether an independent or from a large franchise, the agent should have five years under his or her belt, which is enough time to learn the trade. The agent should be able to provide the names and phones numbers of the buyers (or sellers) of at least five previous sales. Check the references. You'll learn a lot.

5. *Knowledgeable about investment properties:* Many agents know only how to buy and sell property for consumers. You want an agent who knows a good investment when he or she sees one.

Appraisals

Is a formal appraisal the final and best determination of value for a property?

Yes and no. It's important to understand that an appraisal is only a statement of opinion. When made by a professional, it's an educated opinion. But educated people often have different opinions. I've seen two different appraisers come in with appraisals as much as $50,000 apart on a $300,000 home!

If the appraisal is what you hoped it would be, go with it. But if it's far off, then consider getting a second appraisal, a second opinion. If the first and second appraisals are wildly different, you may even want to get yet another, a third opinion!

Buying the First Property

What Type of Property Would Be the Best for Me to Start With?

I'm a first-time investor. What type of real estate should I buy?

Start with a single-family house. There is less risk in single-family home investments than there is with other types of real estate investments, and there are more financing options available (particularly if you intend to occupy it for some time). Look for a newer home to avoid some of the maintenance and repair problems that exist in older homes.

Should I Look for a New Home or a Resale?

Should I buy a brand-new home or a resale when I'm just getting started?

Consider both, and go with the one that offers the best deal at the time. On occasion, brand-new homes can be purchased at bargain prices, but other times the prices are much higher than prices for resales. Buy when new home prices are low, not when they are high.

New homes can be a better buy over the long run because everything works (presumably). Keep in mind, however, that the newness of the house fixtures must be weighed against the number and types of features that may need to be finished, such as fencing, landscaping, and walkways.

Why Should I Buy Investment Property in a Neighborhood with a Low Crime Rate?

Is finding a neighborhood with a low crime rate really important for an investment property? After all, I won't be living there!

The rule is simple: Never buy in a neighborhood where you're afraid to go and collect the rent at any time of the day or night. If you do, you might lose control of the property to gang or hoodlum elements. Vandalism could also be a serious problem, and it could make it difficult to find tenants.

Why Should I Buy Investment Property in a Neighborhood with Good Schools?

Why do you say that schools are so important? Surely tenants, who are probably transient, won't care that much?

All good parents care about their children's education whether they are owners or tenants. Thus, having a good school district is paramount when selecting a property both for renting and for later resale.

While it's true that tenants tend to be more transient than owners, it's not true that they care any less about their children. And having their children in good schools is just as important to them as it is to you.

Yes, you might find a family that will move into a home in a poorly performing school district because they're only going to be there a short time. But you don't want a property that tenants move in and out of all the time. Your clean-up and rent-up costs will be too high in that situation.

Get a property located in a good school district, and it will be both easier to rent and easier to sell.

Should I Buy High-Priced or Low-Priced Property?

Which type of property should I buy: high-priced or low-priced?

To some extent, the answer depends on your financial capabilities and the prevailing market conditions.

Sometimes high-priced properties are quickly moving up in value. If that's the case and you can afford them, that's where the opportunity lies. Other times, the market for high-priced properties is either stagnant or even declining. Stay away.

Interestingly, often when the high end of the market is slow, the lower end may be moving up quickly. It's something to consider.

Comparison Shopping

What is a comparative market analysis (CMA)?

A *comparative market analysis* (CMA) is, as the term suggests, a comparison of comps—that is, properties comparable to the property being considered. When you conduct a CMA, you adjust for differences in features, conditions, locations, and so forth. The result tells you the market value of the property you are considering.

It's important that all the comps you use be recent. Comps over six months old are suspect. Comps over a year old may be useless. In areas where no comps are readily available, you may want to consult with an appraiser to get a *derivative price analysis* from properties that are not quite similar. (A derivative analysis "derives" the price from sales of dissimilar properties.)

Condominium Units versus Single-Family Homes

Should I consider buying a condo as an investment property? I can get one for half the price of a single-family home in my area.

Condos are not simply cheaper single-family homes. They are a different type of lifestyle.

Condos, in general, do not make good rentals. The other owners, through their homeowners' association, often get in the way of acquiring tenants. You may not, for example, be able to put up a sign in the front of the development. Or you may be restricted as to the term you can rent out to tenants.

Also, in general, condos are the last to move up in price during boom periods, and the first to decline during recessions.

If you do decide to go with a condo investment, try to find one in a development where there are few other rentals. Having more than 25 percent rentals in a complex may make it difficult to get financing both when you buy and when you want to resell. It may also drag down the appeal of the development, making it more difficult to get good tenants.

Conversions

From Owner-Occupant to Rental

If I buy a home as an owner-occupant, how long must I live in the property before I can convert it to a rental?

The lender usually wants to be sure that you "intend" to live in the property. Intent is normally demonstrated by moving in and living there. (Of course, you may be prevented from moving in by forces beyond your control, such as a job change or illness.)

I don't know of a hard-and-fast rule that specifies how long you must live in the property before you can safely convert to a rental. Lenders to whom I've spoken, however, suggest that a year is probably a reasonable time. Be sure you check with your attorney before making the decision.

From Rental to Owner-Occupant

How long do I need to rent out a home after a 1031 exchange before I can convert it to my personal residence and resell it claiming the $250,000 capital gains exclusion?

Many investors who have significant capital gains would like to convert a rental to a personal residence and then claim the big exclusion to avoid paying taxes on that gain. There are, however, three steps to the process. The first is typically a 1031 tax-deferred exchange in which the rental is traded for a like-kind home that would be suitable for a personal residence.

The second step is to continue renting out the property for a period of time so that the government can't challenge the 1031 tax-deferred exchange. This is a gray area, and there is no defined time for which you must rent out the property. Accountants with whom

I've spoken, however, have suggested that a year should be enough. Check with your own accountant on this.

Once you move into the house and convert it to a personal residence, however, there's nothing gray about it at all. You must live in the property for two out of five years in order to claim the exemption. That's an additional two years of living in the property.

Only then can you sell and hope to get the up-to-$250,000 ($500,000 for married couples) exclusion. But, as I said, we're talking complex tax maneuvering. You would be wise to check with your own accountant or tax attorney before taking any action. (See also Chapter 12.)

Deposits Accompanying Purchase and Sale Agreements

How long do I have to get my deposit out of a purchase agreement on an investment property? Can I buy contingent on a physical inspection and then back out if I don't like the inspection and still get my deposit back? What if I discover something about the property at the final walk-through? Can I cancel the deal and get my deposit back then?

Most purchase offers boldly state that you are signing a legally binding agreement. If you don't want to buy the house, don't make the offer or agree to the counteroffer. If you do sign, be resigned to the fact that you have bought it. Your deposit is part of your guarantee to purchase.

Having said that, it's important to keep in mind that many states leave "outs" for buyers. For example, California allows three days for the buyer to examine a seller's statement of disclosures about the property. Don't like what the seller discloses within three days? You're usually out of the deal.

Also, a well-written purchase contract will offer the buyer the opportunity to get and approve a professional home inspection report. If you don't like what the report says, disapprove it and you're out. (Some contracts specify that there must be significant problems found for the buyer to get out of the deal.)

Even the federal government allows 10 days' opportunity to have a lead inspection of the property. Find lead and don't approve— again you're out.

This does not, however, usually apply to the final walk-through. Here the point is to provide the buyer the opportunity to see that the house is the same as it was when the offer was made a month or so earlier. Unless there is some new damage or problem found, it's unlikely you can use anything you discover at this time as an out. Indeed, most purchase agreements specifically state that the final walk-through is not to be used as a tool for getting out of the deal.

All of this is moot, however, if the seller decides to challenge. Be sure you check with a good real estate agent or attorney before trying any such ploy. Remember, it's called a *good-faith deposit,* meaning that it is your proof that you intend to go through with the deal. Don't offer it unless you plan to follow through.

Disclosures on the Condition of the Property

When buying a house "as is," is it necessary to get a separate professional inspection, or can I rely on the seller's disclosures?

A professional inspection should be the rule for every investor who's not capable of conducting this inspection himself or herself (which means about 99 percent of the time!). This is especially the case when the seller offers the property as is. Normally sellers don't sell that way unless there's something seriously wrong with the house; offering to sell as is puts most buyers off and often results in a lower sales price That's why most sellers don't use it. On the other hand, it's a real come-on to investors.

It's important to understand that just because a seller offers a property "as is" it doesn't mean he or she does not have to disclose defects. Indeed, disclosure here is doubly important. However, some sellers conveniently forget a few "minor" troubles with the property. While this might provide a course of legal action after the sale, it's always better to get this problem out in the open and dealt with before the deal closes. And a good physical inspection is the right way to attack it.

Financing

Preapprovals

Should I get preapproved if I'm looking to buy a home as an investor?

Yes. And doing so is even more important if you plan to live in your first investment home.

Preapproval is a process whereby a lender looks at your financials and tells you how big a mortgage you can get, and as a result, how big a property you can buy. If you are buying as an owner-occupant, this step is necessary in order to know what you can afford as well as to prove to seller that you have the ability to conclude the purchase.

If you are buying as an investor, this step is necessary in order to know what type of financing is available to you, how much cash you need to put down, and how expensive a property you can afford. The preapproval process for investors who are not intending to live in the property they buy may not be as heavily weighted toward an underwriter's approval and credit scoring, but it is nonetheless, a quick way to determine what a lender will do for you.

Points

What are points?

One point is equal to 1 percent of a mortgage. Two points are 2 percent, and so on. They are tacked onto your closing costs to increase the yield of the mortgage to the lender. You can usually reduce the points (sometimes to zero!) by increasing the interest rate you pay. It's a great way to save money if you're short of cash. Check with your lender as well as Chapter 13.

Creative Financing

I've heard the term "creative financing." What does it mean??

It means any financing that's out of the ordinary course of getting an institutional loan from a lender, such as a bank. For practical purposes it simply means financing that's handled by the seller.

Private Mortgage Insurance (PMI)

Is there any way to avoid the additional cost of private mortgage insurance (PMI) when buying a home with only 10 percent for a down payment?

Any time you get a mortgage for more than 80 percent, the lender is going to want private mortgage insurance (PMI). There is, however, a way to get around it, even when you can afford to put only 10 percent (or less) down. Get an 80 percent mortgage and then a second 10 percent mortgage (putting the remaining 10 percent as cash down). You can expect the second to have a slightly higher interest rate than the first, but the combined rate of the two mortgages should be lower than the combined rate of a big 90 percent mortgage plus PMI. First and second loans are available from institutional lenders.

How do I get the PMI removed on a house I bought to live in a year ago and now want to convert to a rental?

Removing the PMI portion of the loan is of great interest to low-down-payment borrowers as it can shave as much as a hundred dollars or more off the monthly payment. To help borrowers who wish to pursue this course of action, a federal law was passed to require lenders of recent mortgages to remove the PMI when the equity increases to 22 percent of the value. However, in order to get it removed when home prices go up, you must contact your lender and arrange for a new appraisal. Most lenders have a procedure for doing this. Some lenders, however, are a bit slow on the uptake, and it may take several calls and/or letters to get action. Just be sure your equity has, in fact, increased sufficiently, or else you'll just be spinning your wheels.

An alternative may be to refinance to a new mortgage. As long as the loan-to-value ratio (LTV) is 80 percent or less, no PMI is required. No-closing-cost refinancing is widely available, and you should have a good mortgage broker evaluate your current loan to see if going this route makes financial sense for you.

Adjustable-Rate versus Fixed-Rate Mortgages

Where can I find the lowest-cost mortgage? Should I pursue a variable-interest-rate mortgage or a fixed-interest-rate mortgage?

The rule is that you get a fixed-rate mortgage when rates are low to lock them in. You get a variable-rate mortgage when interest rates are high, so that your interest rate will drop as the market comes down. Sometimes in a high-interest-rate market, it can be advisable to try to find a two-step in which, for a small fee, you can convert a variable-rate mortgage to a fixed-rate mortgage after a set period of time, say, two to three years. By then interest rates may be dropping, and you will want to lock in the lower rate.

There are many Web sites through which you can access mortgage brokers and dozens of different financial institutions. Try eloan. com, quicken.com, and mortgage.com. If you don't want to use the Web, consider a mortgage broker in your area. Get a recommendation from a real estate agents. Most good mortgage brokers these days handle dozens of financial institutions.

Fixer-Uppers

Should a Fixer-Upper Be My First Choice As a Real Estate Investment?

Should my first investment property be a fixer-upper?

No. Go with a home in good condition. You'll have enough first-timer problems to deal with without having to worry about renovating the property before you can rent it out.

Fixer-uppers (handyman specials) are great for the experienced investor, someone who knows the ins and outs of real estate transactions and who is handy at fixing things to boot. Extra profits can be made here.

When you're just starting, however, you increase your risks by taking on too much all at once. Stick with just learning to buy and sell. Leave the fixing up for later.

How Do I Evaluate a Run-Down Property?

How do I know if a property will make a good fixer-upper?

It's not hard. But, then again, it's also not easy.

Usually property will be run-down with anything from minor cosmetic blemishes to severe damage. The way to evaluate a property is to make a very accurate calculation of how much it will cost to put the property into tip-top shape. Then find out how much it should

sell for in that final shape and subtract the costs of fixing it up. Also
subtract your own profit and transaction costs. If you can get the
house for the final, low price, it's probably a good deal.

Flipping

Does flipping really work?

Yes, it certainly does! Flipping means that you sell a property as
soon as (or even before!) you take title. It's a way to make big profits very quickly in real estate.

Be aware, however, that flippable properties are few and far
between. This is particularly the case in a slow market. On the other
hand, when the market is boiling over, you can find flippables everywhere.

Check to see if the market is right for flipping properties. You can
ask local agents, or try my test: Check with developers of new homes.
If there are long lines waiting to buy homes, it indicates a market
shortage and strong demand—the fodder right for flipping.

Foreclosures

Where can I find foreclosed properties?

There are many sources. Sometimes people in foreclosure will
advertise for buyers in the local newspaper.

Real estate agents may know of foreclosures. Title insurance and
escrow officers are also good sources.

Lenders advertise properties as part of the foreclosure process in
a local "legal" newspaper. Ask an agent or attorney how to get these
publications as well as bulletins that list such properties.

Inspections

Does Every Investment Property I Buy Need to Be Inspected?

*I'm buying a new home as an eventual investment. Do I need a home
inspection?*

There's a common misconception among new-home buyers that they don't need a home inspection. *Every* home, new or old, should be inspected prior to purchase. Of course, you're more likely to find problems in older homes. But new homes have their share as well. You need a good home inspector who will check out the concrete foundation, the walls and roof, the electrical and plumbing, and all the other home parts for you. Just because it's brand new doesn't mean it was built right.

How Do I Find a Reliable Inspector?

Are there any organizations that regulate home inspectors?

Only a few states regulate home inspectors. However, many inspectors belong to one of the national trade organizations, and many belong to local trade groups as well. The American Society of Home Inspectors (ashi.com, or 800-743-ASHI) offers minimum "standards of practice" that inspectors are expected to follow. You may also want to contact the National Association of Home Inspectors (Nahi.org).

Who Should Do Repairs?

If the sellers disclose or the physical inspection reveals damage that needs to be repaired, is it all right to have the seller do it? Or should I insist that professionals do the job?

When having work done to a roof or anything else in a home as part of a purchase, it's always important to specify in the sales contract that the work must be done in a competent manner up to accepted professional standards. It's a good idea to even specify that it must be done by a professional, not the homeowner. For work that was recently done (and sometimes not so recently), it's also a good idea to request copies of the building permit and the contractor's agreement.

Too often sellers will try to do repair or deferred maintenance work themselves and will botch the job. The result is that it looks bad or it simply does not work (a roof may leak, for example). Better to insist that it be done professionally and not have to worry about it.

Investing

How Much Money Do I Need to Get Started?

Do I need a lot of money to get started investing in real estate?

No. That's a common misconception, probably caused by the fact that property costs so much. Today there's excellent financing that can help you get into your first home. Indeed, if you have a solid job with good income and good credit, you don't need a dime to get started! (See Chapter 13 on financing.)

Should I Live off My Investment Income?

Can I make a living investing in real estate?

Yes, of course. But probably not right away. Never mind what the so-called gurus tell you. When you're getting started as an investor in property, chances are you'll have very little positive cash flow coming to you. Indeed, for a few years you may need to feed those properties—put in money each month just to keep them going!

Real estate investing is a long-term process. After you've been in it for a number of years, your cash flow should increase to the point where you can retire. However, until then it's best done as a part-time business, a few hours a week. In other words, when you're getting started, keep your day job!

Land

Using a Buyer's Broker in Land Purchases

Should I use a buyer's broker when buying rural or bare land?

A buyer's broker will prove invaluable to you if you're inexperienced in land purchases. Undoubtedly the broker will insist that the seller provide a land survey to prove exactly where the land you are buying is located, as well as determine if there are any encroachments. He or she will also check with utility companies to confirm hookups coming to your lot. If the broker is familiar with the area and knows of geological problems, a soils report will be in order. This, of course, is in addition to the usual title report. Finally, the buyer's broker may be able to negotiate a better price or terms for you.

Of course, there is the cost. But, very often a buyer's broker will be able to negotiate with the seller to be paid half the selling commission, in which case your costs would be nothing. (See the section above on Agents.)

Purchasing Bare Land

Bare land and farmland are often advertised at what seem to be very low prices. Are the prices indeed low, and should I take advantage of such apparent bargains?

If I had a chance to purchase a property for $300,000 for which someone else was willing to pay $600,000, I don't think I'd let much stand in the way of my purchase! On the other hand, I've long ago learned that when something sounds too good to be true, it usually is.

Often land that is advertised at a super low price has a problem with it. It might be that there's not enough water, or too much. It could be that the soil is too rocky or too soft for building. It might be that there is simply no power available in the area. Or it could be something else.

My suggestion is that you first consult with a good real estate agent located in the area who knows the type of property and who can tell you what problems are likely to exist. Also, have the agent give you both a written market comparison analysis as well as a thorough appraisal before you buy. This will tell you the property's true value. It will let you know whether you've really got a great deal, or whether you're the subject of a scam.

If, indeed, you can buy land for significantly less than market value, consider flipping. You only need to tie it up and then resell it. You can use a contract in which you have the right to assign the purchase. You can then assign it to another buyer right out of escrow, pocketing your profit. Alternatively, you can try for an option on the property and then sell the option rights to the new buyer, again pocketing your profit. In short, any good real estate attorney should be able to quickly help you make your profit. (Also see Chap. 10.)

Location

Where should I buy my investment rental property?

Always buy it as close to home as possible. Hopefully you'll never own a property that is more than half an hour's drive away. That way you can handle rent-up, respond to tenants' complaints, collect rent, deal with late-payers, and do much of the maintenance and repairs yourself. Long distance is no way to own rental real estate.

Profits

Cashing Out

How do I get my profits out of my investment property?

There are many ways. If you've owned a property for a number of years, chances are your rents have increased to the point where they exceed your expenses. Thus, each month your property pays you.

Of course, you can always sell a property and get your equity out in either cash or paper (a mortgage with you as the lender).

Or you can refinance to get cash out.

Keep in mind, however, that property is not liquid in the financial sense. It's not like a checking or savings account from which you simply demand the money and it's there. That means that while you can get your money out, it can take time to do it—weeks or months (or in a very bad market, sometimes longer). On the other side of the coin, however, the profits are usually far and away superior to anything you can get in a demand money account.

Increasing Profits

How do I increase the profits on an investment property?

Your property will go up in value all on its own because of inflation and the general shortage of most types of real estate in the country (particularly housing). However, you can increase the value of larger types of real estate (apartment houses, commercial and industrial properties, office buildings, and so forth) by increasing the rents. The more rent the property commands, the more it's worth, and the higher a price you can sell it for.

Real-Estate-Owned Properties (REOs)

What is an REO?

A *real-estate-owned property* (REO) is one that a lender, such as a bank, has taken back through foreclosure. The lender is then the owner and typically is anxious to sell. You can often negotiate a good deal with a lender on an REO if you can demonstrate that you have the cash and credit to handle the deal.

You'll have to search to find REOs, however. Lenders are often reluctant to publicize their mistakes (which REOs represent). Sometimes these properties are simply listed with agents. Other times you'll need to call individual lenders and ask. (Also check into Chapter 3.)

Rental Properties

Repairs

How long can I put off a tenant who calls in the middle of the night to say a water heater is broken or a faucet is leaking?

If it's a water heater, you'd better go out right away, even if it is the middle of the night. A leaking water heater can potentially ruin the flooring in a home, if it leaks inside. You'll at least want to get out there to turn off the water (or tell the tenant how to do it). A leaky faucet can wait until morning or the weekend.

It's important, however, to fix all problems with the property as soon as possible. Landlords who refuse (or delay unnecessarily) in remedying problems that affect the habitability of a property may find that the tenants have fixed the problem by calling out an expensive plumber, electrician, or whatever, after which they will have deducted the costs from their rent! Some states provide that tenants have the right to do this, and you just might be up the creek.

Raising Rents

How quickly can I raise rents after I buy a property?

It all depends on the market. If there's a shortage of rental housing and the market goes up quickly, you can raise your rents quickly. Keep in mind, however, that if you raise rents too quickly, your tenants could move out. Be sure to factor in the costs of clean-up and rerenting.

Keep in mind that how much you can charge for rent has nothing whatsoever to do with how much you want or how much your expenses are. It's strictly market driven.

Deposits

Why can't I just keep the cleaning-security deposit? After all, most tenants leave the place in such a mess that some clean-up work is always required.

A cleaning-security deposit must be returned to a tenant who leaves the property in the same condition as it was found, "reasonable wear and tear excepted." That means that there is always going to be some wear and tear on the property including wear to carpets, fading to paint, and so on. These are to be expected no matter who lives in the property, and they are your problem, not the tenants'. However, you can reasonably deduct the cost of repairing deep scratches in the walls or stains on the carpets, for example. What you can and can't subtract is a highly technical matter. Check into Chapter 11 for details.

Most states require that you give an accounting of the security-cleaning deposit to the tenant within 14 to 30 days after they move out explaining how every dime not returned to them was spent.

Selling

Slow-Selling Properties

I can't sell my investment house. I've fixed it up, even put in new carpeting and completely repainted it inside and out. What could be the problem?

Sad to say, but the most common reason for a property not selling is that it's simply priced too high for the current market. If it doesn't sell, immediately get a good comparative market analysis (CMA). Any agent can perform one for you, or you can get it done via the Internet. You need to find out exactly what comparable houses are selling for. If yours is higher, that would explain why it's not selling.

Lease Options

Should an investor seriously consider using a lease option to sell a piece of property?

The lease option has been around for many years, and it is a legitimate method of selling property; however, it's more commonly used in a down market. It involves leasing the property to a hopeful buyer along with an option to buy at a set date and usually at a set price. A portion of each month's rent is applied toward a down payment. At the termination of the lease, when hopefully, the down payment has been reached, the buyer gets a mortgage, and the sale is completed.

With a lease option you can have all the problems inherent in renting including maintenance and the possibility of having to evict the tenant for nonpayment of rent. These risks, however, can be minimized by getting a hefty security deposit and by carefully screening the applicant, making sure that your tenant has a previously successful rental history.

The cause of most problems with lease-option arrangements is that the amount of the rent that goes toward the down payment is not sufficient or the tenant-buyer cannot qualify for a mortgage to complete the purchase when the term of the lease expires. One solution is to get the person preapproved for the eventual financing before renting out the property. In that way you have some assurance that the eventual buyer can qualify for financing; you will also learn just how big a down payment will be needed, and you can adjust the rent accordingly. The problems with this approach are that interest rates fluctuate and people's credit standing changes. The buyer who qualifies today may not tomorrow.

Some experts swear by the lease-option approach. Over the years, however, I have found it to be more bothersome.

Taxes

Deductions

When I buy a property, I understand that I can deduct my mortgage interest and my taxes. Is that a straight one-to-one deduction (a dollar off my taxes for each dollar I spend on interest and taxes)?

No. Confusing a deduction with a credit is a common mistake for first-time investors. What you've described is a credit. What you get is a deduction. That means that on a principal residence, you may be able to offset your income (not your tax liability) by your mortgage interest and taxes. Lower adjusted income, of course, normally results in lower taxes.

On an investment property, you subtract all of your expenses from your rental income. If you have a loss, you might be able to deduct it from your personal income. Check into Chapter 12 for an overview of the tax rules.

I've heard that some investors can't deduct their losses in real estate from their personal income. Is that correct? Why?

It all has to do with the active-passive rules passed by Congress over a decade ago. Very briefly, if your income is above $150,000, then you probably can't deduct any losses from your investment real estate against your personal income in the year they occur. If you earn between $100,000 and $150,000, you can deduct 50 cents in losses for each dollar. If your income is under $100,000, you may be able to deduct up to $25,000 of your loss.

This is a very complex subject, and you shouldn't rely on the very brief explanation given above. Check with your tax attorney or accountant to see how you fare.

Timeshares

Do timeshares make good investments?

No, they usually don't. The truth is that there is a very small resale market for timeshares. When you want to sell, chances are you will find that there are few to no buyers.

On the other hand, I know many people who own and enjoy going to their timeshare each year and who successfully trade for other locations, some in expensive foreign cities. With the price of hotel rooms going up everywhere, timeshares are making more vacation sense than ever before.

Nevertheless, I don't know any timeshare owners who have sold their property for a profit or who have even reached the breakeven point (although I'm sure someone must be out there who has done so). In short, a timeshare doesn't really meet the basic requirement of an investment—that it produce a profit. If you like it, buy it because you'll enjoy it, not because you'll make money on it.

Transaction Costs

I recently bought my first investment property and just as I was going to sign the loan documents, the agent told me there was an additional "transaction cost." Is this legitimate? Do I have to pay it?

Some real estate offices have taken to charging transaction fees to help offset their costs of doing business. It's a way of charging more without actually raising the commission rate. (Sort of like the garbage fees that some lenders charge to increase their yield without increasing the interest rate.)

As a buyer, unless you've previously agreed in writing to pay a transaction cost, you probably don't need to pay it. I don't think it would hurt you to refuse because I can't imagine an agent's dumping a deal for a few hundred dollars.

On the other hand, when it comes time to resell, read the listing agreement carefully from beginning to end. It's a legally binding document. If it contains a clause specifying a transaction fee, you would be bound to pay it.

Index

227

About the Author

Robert Irwin, one of America's leading experts in all areas of real estate, is the author of more than 60 books. His Tips and Traps series for McGraw-Hill has sold over a million copies. A broker and property investor as well as an advisor to consumers and agents, he has helped buyers and sellers solve their real estate investment problems for more than 20 years. He lives in Westlake Village, California. For more real estate tips and traps, go to www.robertirwin.com.